Dear Beautiful Soul

Our Beautiful Qur'an Journey
BOOK 2

by Umm Zakiyyah
and Tadabbur students

Dear Beautiful Soul: Our Beautiful Qur'an Journey
   BOOK 2
by Umm Zakiyyah and Tadabbur students

Tadabbur Authors
Amina H.
Hajara Salihu
Halima Alisa Diallo
Jasmin Umm Jameelah
Kathryn Khadijah Holmes-Adamu
Layla Graham
M. Nation Building
Naimah B
Rasheedah Adisa
Safiyyah Shakir
Shazia Abdullah Ahmed
Umm Maryam
Umm Zakiyyah

UZ Soul Care info at **uzuniversity.com** and **uzhearthub.com**

Arabic script of Qur'an from corpus.quran.com.
English excerpts from the Qur'an are taken from Saheeh
International, Darussalam, and Yusuf Ali translations of
meanings.

Published by Al-Walaa Publications
Gwynn Oak, Maryland USA

Table of Contents

What Is Tadabbur?

The Arabic term *tadabbur* refers to sincere reflection or contemplation and is taken from the *ayah* in the Qur'an that has been translated to mean: *"Do they not then think deeply on the Qur'an, or are their hearts locked up?"* (Muhammad, 47:24).

The Tadabbur program at Our Beautiful Qur'an Journey is taught by Umm Zakiyyah (along with carefully selected UZ Ambassadors and special guests) and is designed for students of all levels. The women who are selected for Tadabbur are committed to connecting to the Qur'an in a way that nourishes their emotional and spiritual health.

The goal of Tadabbur is to inspire lifetime commitment to Qur'an-centered personal improvement in our daily lives, and at Our Beautiful Qur'an Journey, our Tadabbur program is rooted in self-love, self-honesty, and emotional health for the female soul; and the three principles of Tadabbur, as reflected in our weekly journal reflections, are sincerity, humility, and vulnerability.

Find out more at uzhearthub.com.

Preface
Nourishing True Self-Love

Today we hear so much about self-love in discussions of emotional healing and mental wellness. At Our Beautiful Qur'an Journey, we view self-love as rooted in nurturing our spiritual health, which in turn nourishes our emotional and mental wellness. So, for our soul tribe of sisters who come together to study, memorize, and reflect on the Book of Allah, self-love is holistic.

Some time ago, I wrote this reflection in my journal, which encapsulates what self-love means for the UZ Soul Tribe of Our Beautiful Qur'an Journey (Tadabbur):

Reading Qur'an each day is self-love.
Reading Surah Al-Kahf every Friday is self-love.
Praying every Salaah every day on time is self-love.
Spending a few more seconds in sujood is self-love.
Making du'aa for yourself and others is self-love.
Getting up for Qiyaam-ul-Layl each night is self-love.
And being compassionate with yourself—while gently and firmly
*   holding yourself accountable—whenever you fall short in any of*
*   these is self-love.*

As I mention in the preface of Book 1, in Our Beautiful Qur'an Journey, we come together to learn, memorize, and reflect on the Dhikr (the divine message and reminder) that Allah revealed as a gift of guidance to mankind till the end of time. He says:

"Verily We, it is We Who have sent down the Dhikr, and surely, We will guard it [from corruption]."
—*Al-Hijr* (15:9)

Our Merciful Rabb also says:

ٱلَّذِينَ ءَامَنُوا۟ وَتَطْمَئِنُّ قُلُوبُهُم بِذِكْرِ ٱللَّهِ أَلَا بِذِكْرِ ٱللَّهِ تَطْمَئِنُّ ٱلْقُلُوبُ ۝

"Those who believe, and whose hearts find rest (and satisfaction) in the remembrance (dhikr) of Allah, for without doubt in the remembrance of Allah do hearts find rest."
—*Ar-Ra'd* (13:28)

It is the latter *ayah* that is at the heart of this book, a collection of journal excerpts from the students of Tadabbur taken from their weekly entries wherein they write a personal reflection on a Surah or ayah of the Qur'an. Each journal reflection is rooted in the three principles of our Tadabbur program: sincerity, humility, and vulnerability.

Additionally, at the heart of each of these reflections is the foundation of our program itself: self-love, self-honesty, and emotional health for the female soul. I pray our reflections touch your heart and inspire you to draw closer to your Merciful Rabb in this world and in the Hereafter.

Sincerely,

Umm Zakiyyah
November 7th, 2022
13th of Rabee' Ath-Thaani, 1444 AH

For every beautifully imperfect female soul

فَاذْكُرُونِي أَذْكُرْكُمْ وَاشْكُرُواْ لِي وَلَا تَكْفُرُونِ ﴿١٥٢﴾

"So, remember Me; I will remember you. And be grateful to Me and do not deny [My favors upon you]."
—Qur'an (*Al-Baqarah*, 2:152)

PART ONE
Dear Beautiful Soul

1

Cherish Your Beautiful Imperfect Soul
by Umm Zakiyyah

مَا يَفْعَلُ ٱللَّهُ بِعَذَابِكُمْ إِن شَكَرْتُمْ وَءَامَنتُمْ وَكَانَ ٱللَّهُ شَاكِرًا عَلِيمًا ۝

*"What would Allah do with your punishment if you are grateful and
believe? And ever is Allah Appreciative and Knowing."*
—An-Nisaa, 4:147

*D*ear beautiful imperfect soul,
All you can do is the best you can.
No, your best won't be *the* best, but that's okay.
It's the best you can do. And your Merciful Rabb (Lord
and Creator) knows this and still accepts your efforts from
you.

A prophetic teaching that reminds us of this can be
found in the words of a du'aa (prayerful supplication) we
are instructed to say every morning and evening:

*"O Allah, You are my Rabb, none has the right to be worshipped
except You. You created me and I am Your servant, and I abide to
Your covenant and promise as best I can. I take refuge in You from
the evil of which I have committed. I acknowledge Your favor upon
me, and I acknowledge my sin; so forgive me, for verily none can
forgive sin except You"* (Bukhari).

SubhaanAllah, at the very moment we are asking for
forgiveness for falling short in fulfilling our duty to Allah,

we are instructed to say, "I abide to Your covenant and promise as best I can." In these prophetic words, we are reminded that our absolute best will always be imperfect, and that's okay.

So please stop stressing over your faults and sins, even as you continue to strive against them and feel healthy regret. Just continue to show gratefulness to Allah and believe in Him, while trusting that He will not punish you for being an imperfect human. Even on your best days, there's nothing else you can be.

In the Qur'an our Merciful Creator says what has been translated to mean: *"Why should Allah punish you if you have thanked (Him) and have believed in Him? And Allah is Ever All-Appreciative (of good), All-Knowing"* (4:147).

2

Is It Perfection You Seek?
by Umm Maryam

وَبَشِّرِ ٱلْمُؤْمِنِينَ بِأَنَّ لَهُم مِّنَ ٱللَّهِ فَضْلًا كَبِيرًا ﴿٤٧﴾

"And give good tidings to the believers that they will have from Allah great bounty."
—*Al-Ahzaab*, 33:47

Dear beautiful soul,

What are you striving for? Perfection?

The more you strive to make your heart, body, mind, and soul perfect, the more you realize how imperfect you are! The more you realize that it is only Allah who is *Subhanahu wa Ta'ala* (perfect from any imperfections). Yet, He loves you. You, being you. You, being disgraceful. You, being hurtful. You, being ignorant. You, being sinful. He loves you and continuously forgives you!

He chose you to be His '*Ibadi* (worshipper).

Isn't it an honor in and of itself that you get to worship Him, know Him and be with Him at all times?

Why do you chase a mirage when all you need is *sujood* (prostration)? Why do you lose hope in His mercy when He repeatedly introduces Himself as being Ar-Rahman and Ar-Raheem (The Entirely Merciful, The Especially Merciful)?

What are you denying?

You seek the deceptive world and when He deprives you of it because it may harm your soul, you think He will not grant you Paradise?

If He isn't granting you - your desires - to make you stay on the path, why do you think He will abandon you at the dead end?

Remember what Allah says in *Surah Al-Ahzab*:

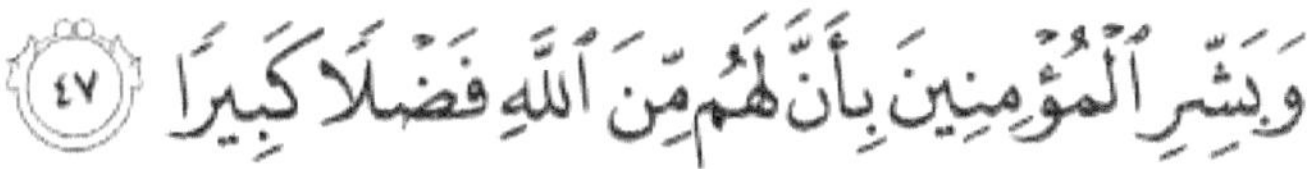

"And give good tidings to the believers that they will have from Allah great bounty" (33:47).

Dear beautiful soul, be compassionate with yourself. You are the servant of the Most Compassionate.

Tawakkul is all you need. Spend your time in *Sabr* and *Shukr* during your layover. Your journey will end soon and you'll see the face of your Lord, the Majestic, inshaAllaah.

And when you think the day is far, remind yourself with what He says in *Surah Ma'aarij*:

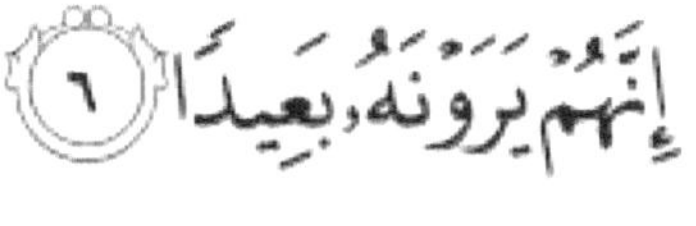

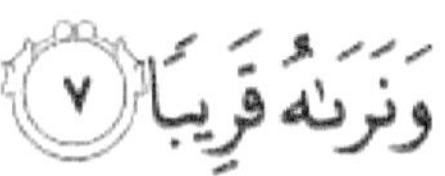

"They see it as far, but We see it as near" (70:6-7).

Do you not see how Allah says it's so near?

Didn't Allah create the heavens and the earth in six days? So, what's the seventh day? Don't you think we are still on day six in Allah's time? What if the Day of Judgment is *the* seventh day?

Dear beautiful soul, ask Allah for the delight of gazing at His Countenance and the eagerness of meeting Him.

3

You've Been Comforted and Embraced
by Umm Jameelah

وَٱعْتَصِمُوا۟ بِحَبْلِ ٱللَّهِ جَمِيعًا وَلَا تَفَرَّقُوا۟ وَٱذْكُرُوا۟ نِعْمَتَ ٱللَّهِ عَلَيْكُمْ إِذْ كُنتُمْ أَعْدَآءً فَأَلَّفَ بَيْنَ قُلُوبِكُمْ فَأَصْبَحْتُم بِنِعْمَتِهِۦٓ إِخْوَٰنًا وَكُنتُمْ عَلَىٰ شَفَا حُفْرَةٍ مِّنَ ٱلنَّارِ فَأَنقَذَكُم مِّنْهَا ۗ كَذَٰلِكَ يُبَيِّنُ ٱللَّهُ لَكُمْ ءَايَٰتِهِۦ لَعَلَّكُمْ تَهْتَدُونَ ﴿١٠٣﴾

"And hold fast, all of you together, to the Rope of Allah (i.e. this Quran), and be not divided among yourselves, and remember Allah's Favor on you, for you were enemies one to another but He joined your hearts together, so that, by His Grace, you became brethren (in Islamic Faith), and you were on the brink of a pit of Fire, and He saved you from it. Thus, Allah makes His Ayat (proofs, pieces of evidence, verses, lessons, signs, revelations, etc.,) clear to you, so that you may be guided."
—Ali 'Imraan, 3:103

Dear beautiful soul whom Allah saved from herself,
Recalling the video I referenced in *I Didn't Want to Become Muslim, Then Snapchat Happened* of how I came to Islam, and the entire experience was my moment of grace.

My moment of being saved by Allah.

My moment was knowing that someone, something was calling me, rather than dragging me to it.

Now, I know it was Allah.

There's a high probability that I was being saved from immense heartbreak, getting pregnant by the wrong person, suicide, you name it.

Most importantly, I was being saved from a *shirk* and *kufr* lifestyle.

I was being saved from what is to come of torture that would have begun my forever (the life of the Hereafter).

O Allah, I thank you for saving me from myself when one more toe, my baby toe, was holding me up from falling into the heat.

The Heat that doesn't care.

Hellfire.

4

The Anesthetic of Emaan
by Layla Graham

فَمَن يُرِدِ ٱللَّهُ أَن يَهْدِيَهُ يَشْرَحْ صَدْرَهُ لِلْإِسْلَٰمِ وَمَن يُرِدْ أَن يُضِلَّهُ يَجْعَلْ صَدْرَهُ ضَيِّقًا حَرَجًا كَأَنَّمَا يَصَّعَّدُ فِى ٱلسَّمَآءِ كَذَٰلِكَ يَجْعَلُ ٱللَّهُ ٱلرِّجْسَ عَلَى ٱلَّذِينَ لَا يُؤْمِنُونَ ۝

"And whomsoever Allah wills to guide, He opens his breast to Islam, and whomsoever He wills to send astray, He makes his breast closed and constricted, as if he is climbing up to the sky. Thus, Allah puts the wrath on those who believe not."
—*Al-An'aam, 6:125*

*D*ear beloved imperfect soul,

You have always trusted Allah, despite your fear and anxiety. When you think back on the hardships in your life, and the ways it has injured you irrevocably, you still know and admit that Allah was, and still is, *Al Haafidh*, The Protector, throughout it all.

He has injected emaan into your heart like an anesthetic to your pain. The trials don't seem as large, as daunting, or as earth-shattering as the sweetness of faith coursing through your veins. As for the sins you've done that you wish you could take back, you *know* deep within yourself that without those faults and sins, you wouldn't have spent as much time beseeching Allah.

You have seen miracles happen when you've been humble enough to plead. And you've been comforted and embraced when you thought you were alone. So be faithful and steadfast. Know that your Rabb is *Al Wadud, Al Lateef.* The Most Loving, The Gentle.

5

I Fear Losing My Way
by Halima Alisa Diallo

۞ لَتُبْلَوُنَّ فِى أَمْوَٰلِكُمْ وَأَنفُسِكُمْ وَلَتَسْمَعُنَّ مِنَ ٱلَّذِينَ أُوتُوا۟ ٱلْكِتَٰبَ مِن قَبْلِكُمْ وَمِنَ ٱلَّذِينَ أَشْرَكُوٓا۟ أَذًى كَثِيرًا ۚ وَإِن تَصْبِرُوا۟ وَتَتَّقُوا۟ فَإِنَّ ذَٰلِكَ مِنْ عَزْمِ ٱلْأُمُورِ ۝١٨٦

"You shall certainly be tried and tested in your wealth and properties and in your personal selves, and you shall certainly hear from those who received the Scripture before you and from those who ascribe partners to Allah much abuse, but if you persevere patiently, and become Al-Muttaqun (the pious; people of taqwaa) then verily, that will be a determining factor in all affairs, and that is from the great matters [which you must hold on with all your efforts]."
—*Ali 'Imraan*, 3:186

Dear beautiful imperfect soul,

I fear losing my way and at times it's scary. I feel as though I have to carry the burden of my soul due to spiritual self-deception, even though my Merciful Rabb is with me on this path.

I feel like I was created to endure trials no matter what. And no matter how hard I try to see the good in myself and others, the 48 years I have lived on this earth by Allah's mercy and grace, have shown me that people are toxic.

I have found that people are not as nice, caring, loving, or humble as in the past. I say this because most of the people I interact with daily are non-Muslims. I try to respect them for who they are and not for who they are not. It is a humane thing to respect others. But I have come to see that even those I try to respect and see the good in - those who have humane issues just like me - suddenly have a hidden agenda that was unexpected.

It makes me feel uncomfortable at times to be in their company. I pray to Allah to guide me to set boundaries, so I don't feel uncomfortable. I know it is because of the spiritual wounding that I feel like this.

I feel that because I am Muslim, I should feel comfortable within myself and not allow the different lifestyles or beliefs of others to be a conflict of interest. I don't want to fall into spiritual self-deception and whatever others do in their lives, because that is their business.

I am only responsible for myself and what I choose to do and not do, as these are the actions that will determine my final home: Heaven or Hell.

6

The Ways of the Universe
by Halima Alisa Diallo

إِنَّ فِى خَلْقِ ٱلسَّمَوَتِ وَٱلْأَرْضِ وَٱخْتِلَفِ ٱلَّيْلِ وَٱلنَّهَارِ وَٱلْفُلْكِ ٱلَّتِى تَجْرِى فِى ٱلْبَحْرِ بِمَا يَنفَعُ ٱلنَّاسَ وَمَآ أَنزَلَ ٱللَّهُ مِنَ ٱلسَّمَآءِ مِن مَّآءٍ فَأَحْيَا بِهِ ٱلْأَرْضَ بَعْدَ مَوْتِهَا وَبَثَّ فِيهَا مِن كُلِّ دَآبَّةٍ وَتَصْرِيفِ ٱلرِّيَحِ وَٱلسَّحَابِ ٱلْمُسَخَّرِ بَيْنَ ٱلسَّمَآءِ وَٱلْأَرْضِ لَأَيَتٍ لِّقَوْمٍ يَعْقِلُونَ ﴿١٦٤﴾

"Indeed, in the creation of the heavens and earth, and the alternation of the night and the day, and the [great] ships which sail through the sea with that which benefits people, and what Allah has sent down from the heavens of rain, giving life thereby to the earth after its lifelessness and dispersing therein every [kind of] moving creature, and [His] directing of the winds and the clouds controlled between the heaven and the earth are signs for a people who use reason."
—*Al-Baqarah*, 2:164

Dear beautiful hurting soul,
I know you wonder about the ways of the Universe. You wonder what it was before it became a world, country, or nation. Was it just soil and rocks? Were there planets and orbits? Was there any flowing water, trees, or mountains? Or is it just my imagination running away with me?

Dear beautiful hurting soul, when I look up at the sky and see the clouds, birds, rain, sun, and snow, I know there is a magnificent miracle that is beyond my comprehension. And all I can do is trust the process as time goes on.

Yes, I am afraid, beautiful hurting soul, of all the evil and chaos that is occurring around the world.

Yes, I am afraid, beautiful hurting soul, about where my final destination will be.

Yes, I am sometimes sad, beautiful hurting soul, of all I had to endure and will endure in my lifetime.

Dear beautiful hurting soul, I know I should not feel that what I endured growing up and did not understand why, was a punishment. I just felt at times that it was a phase I had to go through and eventually things would get better.

But dear beautiful hurting soul, throughout it all Allah made a way when there seemed to be no way. When I felt that not being here was the best solution for everyone including myself, Allah saw different. He caused the pills I took to come out of my body. I think that was a sign that it is okay.

Dear beautiful hurting soul, I know you are hurting. I know this is not what you expected your life to be like. Be patient. Heal from all the hurting. Never give up on the mercy, forgiveness, and compassion of your Lord. He knows what you are going through but trust and believe in him.

Believe in the process, my dear beautiful hurting soul. It will be okay.

7

Thank You, Dear Beautiful Soul
by Hajara Salihu

وَإِذْ تَأَذَّنَ رَبُّكُمْ لَئِن شَكَرْتُمْ لَأَزِيدَنَّكُمْ وَلَئِن كَفَرْتُمْ إِنَّ عَذَابِي لَشَدِيدٌ ﴿٧﴾

"And [remember] when your Lord proclaimed, 'If you are grateful, I will surely increase you [in favor]; but if you deny, indeed, My punishment is severe.'"
—Ibraaheem, 14:7

Dear beautiful soul,
Thank You!
For all the times you allowed yourself to cry.
For getting up when you fell
For being strong on the days you felt so weak.
Thank you for keeping this soul together.
You're strong not because you look it, or because you don't have fears.
You're strong because you've looked fear in the eye, walked through it, and came out better.
Thank you for your unwavering faith. For your firm belief in the certainty of your Lord's Promise, Mercy, and Blessings.
This will carry you through.
Your Merciful Rabb hasn't forgotten you.

He will preserve for you, the reward for every pain you've felt. He will let you taste the sweetness of your patience in this *dunya* and the Hereafter.

Your Lord will keep raising your rank in *Jannah* as you pass through your trials with patience and perseverance.

Dear Beautiful Soul, everything is well with you. In shaa Allah.

8

You Are Loved, Dear Sister
by Layla Graham

إِنَّ فِى خَلْقِ ٱلسَّمَـٰوَٰتِ وَٱلْأَرْضِ وَٱخْتِلَـٰفِ ٱلَّيْلِ وَٱلنَّهَارِ لَـَٔايَـٰتٍ لِّأُو۟لِى ٱلْأَلْبَـٰبِ ﴿١٩٠﴾

ٱلَّذِينَ يَذْكُرُونَ ٱللَّهَ قِيَـٰمًا وَقُعُودًا وَعَلَىٰ جُنُوبِهِمْ وَيَتَفَكَّرُونَ فِى خَلْقِ ٱلسَّمَـٰوَٰتِ وَٱلْأَرْضِ رَبَّنَا مَا خَلَقْتَ هَـٰذَا بَـٰطِلًا سُبْحَـٰنَكَ فَقِنَا عَذَابَ ٱلنَّارِ ﴿١٩١﴾

*"Verily! In the creation of the heavens and the earth, and in the
alternation of night and day, there are indeed signs for men of
understanding. Those who remember Allah (always, and in prayers)
standing, sitting, and lying down on their sides, and think deeply
about the creation of the heavens and the earth, (saying): 'Our Lord!
You have not created (all) this without purpose, glory to You!
(Exalted be You above all that they associate with You as partners).
Give us salvation from the torment of the Fire.'"*
—Ali 'Imraan, 3:190-191

To my beautiful sister in faith and struggle,
I struggle to convey in words what my heart
needs you to understand.
Allah never needed us.
Allah never needed human beings to exist and for us to
worship Him. Allah is self-sufficient in the actual sense of

the word. Quite literally He does not need any of our du'as, salawat, tasbeeh, recitation, deeds—any of it.

But here we are. Many of us feel the hardship of this world closing in on us from every side and think I never asked to be born, or, I never asked to exist. And we feel pity for ourselves in the pain we must endure to just live life as human beings.

But Allah created us and we get to experience the privilege of worshiping the One True God. I don't think we truly comprehend the gravity and enormity of our existence. We get to have a relationship with **God**. We get to pray, bow down, and prostrate to the same Creator that hung the stars and anchored the mountains.

Have you ever seen those videos that simulate the vastness of the multiverse, where they zoom out the camera from the earth, and we see the earth's size in comparison to the other planets, our sun, and the size of the solar system? Then it zooms out more to show stars that share the same galaxy as ours, and then it shows the milky way.

Have you seen the earth or even our one star in comparison to Antares (883 times the mass of the sun and 550 light years away) or RW Cephei (1,535 times the mass of the sun and 3,500 light years away)? Our human brains and eyes have difficulty comprehending the size and distance of these massive celestial creations and yet we share the same God. We share the same Creator.

And those mighty stars worship Him too. Black holes don't form except by His permission. An acorn doesn't fall from a tree except with His notice. You don't involuntarily blink without Allah commanding your body to do so.

How great is that? It makes our temporary pain and struggles seem less burdensome because the same God that is taking care of the multiverse is taking care of you too, my dear sister.

You're loved. By Rabbal Alameen.

Ugh. I can't even think this without feeling my heart hammer in my chest. Allahu Akbar.

Don't fret, fellow worshiper. Say Alhamdulillah for your existence. Say Alhamdulillah for being in submission to Allah willingly. Say Alhamdulillah for being the creation of a Lord that is Al Aleem, The All-Aware, Al Khabeer, The All-Knowing.

Say Alhamdulillah and rejoice.

9

Your Rabb Will Never Forsake You
by Layla Graham

بِسْمِ اللَّهِ الرَّحْمَٰنِ الرَّحِيمِ

وَالضُّحَىٰ ﴿١﴾

وَاللَّيْلِ إِذَا سَجَىٰ ﴿٢﴾

مَا وَدَّعَكَ رَبُّكَ وَمَا قَلَىٰ ﴿٣﴾

"By the Glorious Morning Light, and by the Night when it is still, your Guardian-Lord has not forsaken you, nor is He displeased."
—Ad-Duhaa, 93:1-3

ear beautiful hurting soul,

Being hurt and betrayed by people and the community that is supposed to have your back has shattered you. It deeply broke your faith in the Ummah and your trust in them. It has led to so much turmoil in your heart and caused feelings of animosity towards them.

This has led to a weakening of your spirit because you struggled to reconcile their behavior with the core truth of Islam.

But since then you've learned that the behavior of human beings does not reflect the perfection, love, and mercy of your Creator.

Allah is The Most Just and will never forsake you.

10

With Allah, Nothing Is a Loss
by Layla Graham

مَن ذَا ٱلَّذِى يُقْرِضُ ٱللَّهَ قَرْضًا حَسَنًا فَيُضَٰعِفَهُۥ لَهُۥ وَلَهُۥٓ أَجْرٌ كَرِيمٌ ﴿١١﴾

"Who is it that would loan Allah a goodly loan so He will multiply it for him and he will have a noble reward?"
—Al-Hadeed, 57:11

Dear beautiful imperfect soul,

Remember when you gave $50 for sadaqah as a little girl when you were first learning about charity and selflessness? Your heart wanted to give but your mind mourned those $50.

But then, only minutes after giving away that money, your father found a $50 bill in the street and gave it to you. You stood there, eyes wide, staring at the money in your hand, feeling awe and wonder.

Since then, you've had full faith that Allah is always with those who do good deeds for His sake and that He will *always* take care of you.

11

The Secret Medicine of Qur'an
by Hajara Salihu

وَلَنَبْلُوَنَّكُم بِشَىْءٍ مِّنَ ٱلْخَوْفِ وَٱلْجُوعِ وَنَقْصٍ مِّنَ ٱلْأَمْوَٰلِ وَٱلْأَنفُسِ وَٱلثَّمَرَٰتِ وَبَشِّرِ ٱلصَّٰبِرِينَ ﴿١٥٥﴾

"And We will surely test you with something of fear and hunger and a loss of wealth and lives and fruits, but give good tidings to the patient."
—*Al-Baqarah*, 2:155

My *dear beloved sister,*
I am writing you this letter in hopes and belief that you are well *in shaa Allah.*

My words to you today go beyond any difference we may have, whether of race, nationality, or tribe. Islam is a gift we both share and as such, I owe you my words of compassion, kindness, and love.

I don't know and can't imagine how exactly you're feeling or what you're passing through. But I want to let you know that you're not alone in this and your feelings are valid.

Here's a little secret. I've found the Qur'an to be medicinal. Therein, I have found the answers to questions that have lingered for so long on my mind. Go to it. You'll feel relaxed in solitude.

Just you and your Merciful Rabb. Tell it all to Him, let the tears flow, and when you run out of words, stay still and calm. Your Lord knows what's in your heart.

They say the food of the soul is *Dhikr*. Feed your soul with the remembrance of Allah. Glorify Him, praise Him, and seek His aid. Expression of gratitude is another way to keep you grounded. Keep a gratitude journal. Thank Allah for everything. Even your trials.

I know you have lots of doubts and so many questions you want to ask. I know you have asked so many times when the help of Allah will arrive. Remember, the trials we face are means to test our emaan and earn a reward as Allah says [what has been translated to mean]:

"And We will surely test you with something of fear and hunger and a loss of wealth and lives and fruits but give good tidings to the patient" (2:155).

I don't know how you bear these trials with patience, but I know it is hard. Here's my word to you:

Hold on with firm resolve that Allah alone is your Helper. Remember that His mercy encompasses His wrath. Have good thoughts about Allah and know that Allah's help is near.

The Prophet (peace be upon him) said: *"The Muslims in their mutual love, kindness, and compassion are like the human body where when one of its parts is in agony the entire body feels the pain, both in sleeplessness and fever"* (Bukhari and Muslim).

This is me in mutual love, kindness, and compassion. I hope you treat yourself to some too. I leave you in Allah's care.

Your sister in love and faith.

PART TWO
Alone with Your Lord

12

Be Prepared to Be Alone
by Umm Zakiyyah

وَلَئِن سَأَلْتَهُم مَّنْ خَلَقَ ٱلسَّمَٰوَٰتِ وَٱلْأَرْضَ لَيَقُولُنَّ ٱللَّهُ قُلْ أَفَرَءَيْتُم مَّا تَدْعُونَ مِن دُونِ ٱللَّهِ إِنْ أَرَادَنِيَ ٱللَّهُ بِضُرٍّ هَلْ هُنَّ كَٰشِفَٰتُ ضُرِّهِ أَوْ أَرَادَنِي بِرَحْمَةٍ هَلْ هُنَّ مُمْسِكَٰتُ رَحْمَتِهِ قُلْ حَسْبِيَ ٱللَّهُ عَلَيْهِ يَتَوَكَّلُ ٱلْمُتَوَكِّلُونَ ﴿٣٨﴾

"And if you asked them, 'Who created the heavens and the earth?'
they would surely say, 'Allah.' Say, 'Then have you considered what
you invoke besides Allah? If Allah intended me harm, are they
removers of His harm, or if He intended me mercy, are they
withholders of His mercy?' Say, 'Sufficient for me is Allah; in Him
those who trust must put their trust."
—*Az-Zumar,* 39:38

Dear struggling soul,
    Be prepared to be alone.
No one can do your soul-work on your behalf.
No one.

So, if you sincerely want to meet Allah with emaan in your heart, be prepared to be alone.

But know, though you are alone, you are in the company of Allah.

13

So, Where Are You Going?
by Umm Zakiyyah

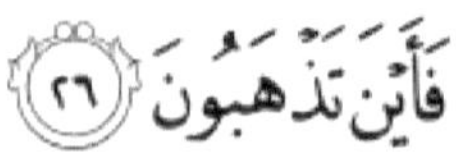

"So where are you going?"
—*At-Takwir*, 81:26

*D*ear *hurting soul,*
Know this.
Allah created the human soul such that it will never find complete rest and satisfaction in this world.

The closest a human being can get to genuine worldly happiness and contentment is sincerely and consistently nourishing the soul. And this can only be achieved through humble and continuous submission to our Merciful Creator.

In this, Salaah becomes the life of our soul, Qur'an becomes the spring of our heart, and Qiyaam al-Layl (the Night Prayer) becomes the coolness of our eye.

If you seek fulfillment in this world through anything that is not rooted in these three sources of spiritual nourishment, then your heart will forever be chasing an ever-elusive mirage of happiness.

14

Remember, This Is a Gift of Honor
by Naimah B.

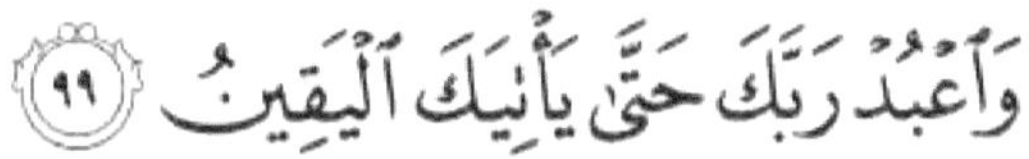

"And worship your Lord until there comes to you the certainty (death)."
—*Al-Hijr*, 15:99

Dear soul seeking blessings and forgiveness,
Look at how Allah has lifted you up, chosen you to know and worship Him while many are still lost. Look at how He protected your innocent mind from the acceptance of shirk at such an early age.

Remember that this is a gift of honor.

Allah created us in the best form, with the ability to choose and endure tests. And at the same time, He provided us with an answer key. Informing us of the consequences behind our decisions. Giving us a clear vision of what the good and bad of them look like. Knowing that honestly, we are a ticking time bomb, and upon the explosion, what we did and how we lived will determine our eternal end.

Allah promises an excellent celebration for the best choices, through the toughest circumstances for the purest hearts.

Remember to examine the true enemy, Shaytaan, and guard your soul against his trickery. Don't forget to ask Allah for His help, to follow the answer key, because that is the rope. This is the recipe for having your final celebration in eternal bliss.

I know there are times when it can feel like you missed the mark, but Allah told us to seek His forgiveness and try our very best because Indeed He knows the best.

So, if you were chosen from amongst the rest, be intentional about your worship so the rewards can manifest.

15

My Therapy Sessions with Allah: On Anxiety and Feeling Alone
by Rasheedah Adisa

إِنَّمَا يُؤْمِنُ بِـَٔايَٰتِنَا ٱلَّذِينَ إِذَا ذُكِّرُواْ بِهَا خَرُّواْ سُجَّدًا وَسَبَّحُواْ بِحَمْدِ رَبِّهِمْ وَهُمْ لَا يَسْتَكْبِرُونَ ۩ ﴿١٥﴾

تَتَجَافَىٰ جُنُوبُهُمْ عَنِ ٱلْمَضَاجِعِ يَدْعُونَ رَبَّهُمْ خَوْفًا وَطَمَعًا وَمِمَّا رَزَقْنَٰهُمْ يُنفِقُونَ ﴿١٦﴾

فَلَا تَعْلَمُ نَفْسٌ مَّآ أُخْفِيَ لَهُم مِّن قُرَّةِ أَعْيُنٍ جَزَآءًۢ بِمَا كَانُواْ يَعْمَلُونَ ﴿١٧﴾

"Only those believe in Our verses who, when they are reminded by them, fall down in prostration and exalt [Allah] with praise of their Lord, and they are not arrogant. Their sides forsake their beds, to invoke their Lord in fear and hope, and they spend [charity] out of what We have bestowed on them. And no soul knows what has been hidden for them of comfort for eyes as reward for what they used to do."
—As-Sajdah, 32:15-17

I watched everything I held onto leave one after another.

I heard the false accusations and slander.

I unassumingly saw the last person take their exit.
And for the first time, I realized I was truly and completely
alone.

The first night was the hardest
The darkness of the night and my new room slightly
scaring me
Did I lock the door right?
How will I survive tonight? I wonder
The tears start to trickle as I stare into my phone,
"There was really nobody to call."
"There was really nobody who could understand
the depth of my feelings."

My head now pounding from all the tears and confusion,
I begin to mumble
I begin to mumble to Allah for help
Slowly at first
And then more intently
I begin to beg for help and relief.

One night after another
The Night prayer became my escape
And Istighfar, the strategy
Al Fatiha, my oft repeated
Allah, my true companion
And the darkness that once used to scare me, now
becoming my covering.

Unburdening all the weight one day after another
Begging Him each day for clarity and guidance
Telling Him the intentions and truths no one else wanted
to hear
Acknowledging my wrong and begging for mercy

Feeling the sakeenah (soul-nourishing tranquility) in my
heart with every word I utter
Watching the strength return I know only Him could give.
Words simply do not do justice.

And so when every lover is with their lover,
When every friend is with their friend,
When everyone is with their chosen,
Know that you have one in Allah too!
His hands are ever opened to receive you.
He is ever waiting for you to return to Him.
And He descends every single night, asking about YOU!
Yes you, dear soul!
Yes, you!
So, don't delay
Even if all you do today is make or renew the intention
It is truly a special time
And words simply do not do justice
Remember - *No soul can imagine what delights are kept in
store for them as a reward for what they used to do.*

16

Check Your Intention
by Safiyyah Shakir

لَّا يُؤَاخِذُكُمُ ٱللَّهُ بِٱللَّغْوِ فِىٓ أَيْمَـٰنِكُمْ وَلَـٰكِن يُؤَاخِذُكُم بِمَا كَسَبَتْ قُلُوبُكُمْ ۗ وَٱللَّهُ غَفُورٌ حَلِيمٌ ﴿٢٢٥﴾

"Allah will not hold you accountable for unintentional oaths, but for what you intended in your hearts. And Allah is All-Forgiving, Most Forbearing."
—Al-Baqarah, 2:225

I must begin my first entry with this *ayah* as there is a story I would like to share. In 2021, the first *Taddabur* book project was started and completed. I had every intention to submit a few entries for the first project.

However, I was skeptical. Not of the project, mind you, but of my own intentions. I didn't want to write and get published for attention. I wanted my intentions to be purely on my writing being a benefit to someone else as well as myself. So each time I sat down to write, I made du'aa to Allah to allow me to write only if my intentions were pure. And each time something took me away from my writing.

1. I would forget what I was going to write
2. I started doing something else
3. Someone needed me for something
4. It was late and I needed to sleep

There were so many instances of me being pulled away from writing, that I finally said, "Ok. I'll wait until the next time In Sha Allah." In that way, the opportunity to share

my thoughts and journey as a struggling soul was taken
from me. Again, I sit down to write and pray the same
du'aa again. I pray that He guides my pen as I write on
paper and my fingers as I type on my laptop, to only speak
the truth.

17

Preparing for the Blessed Month of Ramadan
by Safiyyah Shakir

بِسْمِ ٱللَّهِ ٱلرَّحْمَٰنِ ٱلرَّحِيمِ

إِنَّآ أَنزَلْنَٰهُ فِى لَيْلَةِ ٱلْقَدْرِ ﴿١﴾

وَمَآ أَدْرَىٰكَ مَا لَيْلَةُ ٱلْقَدْرِ ﴿٢﴾

لَيْلَةُ ٱلْقَدْرِ خَيْرٌ مِّنْ أَلْفِ شَهْرٍ ﴿٣﴾

تَنَزَّلُ ٱلْمَلَٰئِكَةُ وَٱلرُّوحُ فِيهَا بِإِذْنِ رَبِّهِم مِّن كُلِّ أَمْرٍ ﴿٤﴾

سَلَٰمٌ هِىَ حَتَّىٰ مَطْلَعِ ٱلْفَجْرِ ﴿٥﴾

*'Indeed, We sent it [the Qur'an] down during the Night of Decree.
And what can make you know what is the Night of Decree?
The Night of Decree is better than a thousand months. The angels
and the Spirit descend therein by permission of their Lord for every
matter. Peace it is until the emergence of dawn.'*
—*Al-Qadr*, 97:1-5

On April 24th, 2022, Ustadha held one last *Taddabur* class for the month of Ramadan. During this class, she talked about the virtues of *Laylatul-Qadr*, how to benefit from *Laylatul-Qadr*, and how to properly take advantage of every night to witness *Laylatul-Qadr*. At the end of the lesson, we were given time to write in our journals from one of the prompts Ustadha had given us. One of the prompts that stood out to me stated the following:

"Now that Ramadan is nearly coming to a close, do you feel you have taken advantage of this Blessed Month as much as you could?"
I responded to the prompt with the following:

It's not that I don't feel like I have taken advantage of this Blessed Month as best as I could. I know that I have not. I look back on the days that I wasted. Days that, had I put in the work, maybe I could have gained blessings and started the process of changing who I am as a person. Instead, all I see are wasted days listening to my nafs. So much so that had other temptations been put back in my life I would have gone and said "hey, how you doin?" without any prompting from any whispers.

That is how misguided my soul is, that is how bad I have transgressed against myself. That is how deep I am in this world of sinning and how scared I am for my soul during its journey in the grave and the Barazaq. However, Allah has showered me with many blessings this month. So many that I wish tears would fall from my eyes. Has this blessing been taken from me? Or is there not enough proper Tawakkal in my heart? I spoke to my soul tribe about my biggest struggles at work. But was it a struggle for me or did it become a true struggle once I spoke to my beautiful sisters? How great is Allah's will?

Though Ramadan of 1443 is over, Ramadan of 1444 is just around the corner. Praise be to Allah the Greatest! The excitement in me to see Ramadan again mirrors that which I felt when I was a child. When the excitement of seeing this holy month was still of pure innocence and truly understanding the significance of this holy month. There is a Hadith that mentions how the Sahabah would get ready for Ramadan six months before its arrival.

So here I am getting ready.

I am preparing for the many trials and tribulations that come with Ramadan.

I am preparing for long nights of worship.

I am preparing for the battle of eating only what I need and not bloating my stomach past what it can sustain.

I am preparing for the struggle of drinking the daily amount of water needed for me to stay hydrated.

I am preparing for completing a Khatam; reading the entire Quran from beginning to end in Arabic

I am preparing for reading the entire Quran in English

I am preparing myself to be open to the naked truths about my nafs; my soul.

More importantly, I am preparing myself for the hard work needed to see the blessings of Ramadan and gain the favor of Allah.

Ya Allah, I thank you for the blessing of Ramadan.

Ya Allah, I thank you for the blessing of Ramadan.

Ya Allah, I thank you for the blessing of Ramadan.

Ya Allah, I ask that you grant me and everyone who reads this entry the ability to see the blessed month of Ramadan again. I ask that you allow us to be shown our true selves during this month and that you open our hearts to that naked truth so that we may begin and continue to work on ourselves and better our imperfect selves in a way that is pleasing to you and allows us to be in good standing

with you until the day we stand before you to receive our
Book in our right hand.

18

Allah Intends Good for You
by M. Nation Building

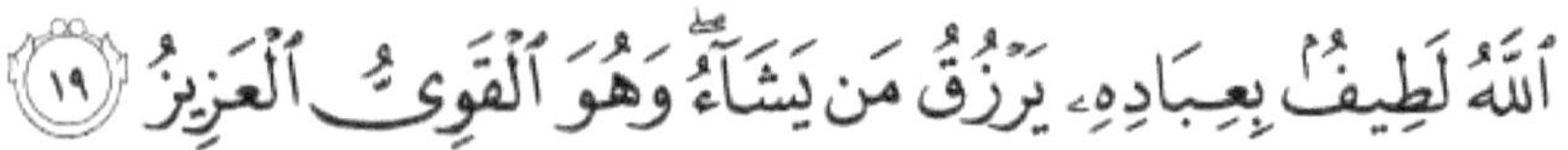

*"Allah is very Gracious and Kind to His slaves. He gives provisions
to whom He wills. And He is the Powerful, the Exalted in Might."*
—*Ash-Shooraa*, 42:19

Allah intends good for you and Allah's promise is always true. These words echo comfort like a warm embrace on the coldest of days. As human beings, we are naturally reassured by the concept of anyone intending good for us. It creates an ease that allows us to let our guard down and develop a deeper trust with that individual. What if that was then topped with the guarantee that their word is bonded; that they are true to their trust and honor their word? Our loyalty to that individual would be unwavering, due to the value and protection we experience within that relationship. We would earnestly protect and nurture that relationship. If this is the case with our human connections that often fluctuate - because truly we human beings fall short, prone to error, and let one another down - what should this say about the powerful connection Allah is offering to the human believing soul?

Allah, who is without fault. Whose promise is always true and never falters. Who consistently tells us to turn to Him and that He is near. He is our source of comfort and peace. *As for those who repent, believe, and do good deeds, they are the ones whose evil deeds Allah will change into good deeds. For Allah is All-Forgiving, Most Merciful.* - Furqan 25:70

Thinking of my Lord telling me specifically as a servant who makes mistakes offers *Tauba* and prays that He accepts it, who believes in Him, and who strives to do my best even when I fall short, the thought of my Lord saying for you, I will change your evil deeds into good.

Of course, this is with sincerity of the heart and intentions upright. Personalizing Allah's promises, and thinking good of my Lord, is a source of healing from all the ways I was taught of fearing Allah's wrath over trusting in Allah's mercy and promises to the doer of good.

Allah loves the doer of good. How did I miss the lesson on Allah's love?

Yes, we MUST do our part, but to miss the mercy over being so frozen by fear, seeming to bypass every opening of every Sura (except one), that guides the human heart and soul to ponder upon and remember that indeed your Lord is Most Gracious, Most Merciful.

I want my soul to remember Allah's capacity to dispense true justice and consequences for our persistent defiance, but I never want to lose the comforting embrace of Allah setting us up for success.

Whoever comes with a good deed will be rewarded tenfold. But whoever comes with a bad deed will be punished for only one. None will be wronged. - *Al- Anaam 6:160*

Not only does Allah promise to multiply our good, and count our evil as just one, but He (Azwajaal) promises that no soul shall be wronged. In the least.

This verse fills me with such humble gratitude for the mercy of our Lord, that He would multiply the good we do, and count our evil as just that, then reassure us, we a people that has suffered so much injustice by the hand of human beings, that *no soul shall be wronged in the least.*

"But seek, through that which Allah has given you, the home of the Hereafter; and [yet], do not forget your share of the world. And do good as Allah has done good to you."-Al-Qasas 28:77
He calls us back to Him, encouraging us to seek our home in the hereafter, through the good He (Az wajaal) continuously guides us toward. Blessing us with an opportunity to face tests and trials in this life that draw us nearer to Him, trading the very temporary sacrifice in this life, for a permanent abode in the hereafter. None of us can be worthy of such forgiveness and mercy, and yet Allah still offers it to us, while He also commands us "and [yet], do not forget your share of the world." Reminding us not to forget our portion of the *Dunya*. Don't forget your needs and pleasures here, even as you strive for your ultimate home in the hereafter. This home-calling brings tears to my eyes as I reflect upon the most nurturing presence in our physical world here now, which is our mothers. Whenever I would get swamped with work or seem to allow my tasks to get ahead of me, my mother would tell me "Do not forget to take care of your needs as you are in service to others."
"Do not forget your portion." It is such a loving command. Do the work you must, to safeguard and build

in the hereafter, but do not forget your portion before you here and now. Rasulullah (s.a.w) said

"Allah is more merciful to His servants than a mother is to her child." (Ṣaḥīḥ al-Bukhārī & Muslim)

So, reminding my soul of this mercy, compassion, and promise, allow me to naturally regulate the faith-based fear of losing the peace and grace of a Lord most gracious and most merciful.

19

Vision
by Aminah H.

كَيْفَ تَكْفُرُونَ بِاللَّهِ وَكُنتُمْ أَمْوَاتًا فَأَحْيَاكُمْ ثُمَّ يُمِيتُكُمْ ثُمَّ يُحْيِيكُمْ ثُمَّ إِلَيْهِ تُرْجَعُونَ ٢٨

"How can you disbelieve in Allah when you were lifeless and He brought you to life; then He will cause you to die, then He will bring you [back] to life, and then to Him you will be returned."
—Al-Baqarah, 2:28

"Indeed Allah, the Blessed and Exalted, created His creation in darkness, then He cast His Light upon them, so whoever is touched by that light is guided, and whoever is not, goes astray" [Jami At Tirmithi 26:42].

Vision is an important thing. Without vision, you cannot see your way. I continue to strive for the vision of the heart as it is so much more important. As I experience

o The anxiety
o The sadness
o The disappointment
o The hope
o The strength
o The love
o The wanting
o The neglect

o   The errors
o   The lies
o   The Truth
o   The commitment
o   The joy
o   The agony
o   The wishes
o   The faith
o   The caring
o   The loving too much
o   The loving too little
o   The nurturing
o   The deception
o   The dreams
o   The aspirations
o   The goals
o   The visions
o   The fear

There, buried in all the darkness is light. A bright light that commands …. Allahu Akbar.

A light that says, I am still here waiting for you.

20

Do You Want to Be Close to Your Merciful Rabb?

by Hajara Salihu

نَتَجَافَىٰ جُنُوبُهُمْ عَنِ ٱلْمَضَاجِعِ يَدْعُونَ رَبَّهُمْ خَوْفًا وَطَمَعًا وَمِمَّا رَزَقْنَٰهُمْ يُنفِقُونَ

"They arise from [their] beds; they supplicate their Lord in fear and aspiration, and from what We have provided them, they spend."
—*As-Sajdah, 32:16*

What does it take to be close to Allah?

"*The closest a servant is to ar-Rabb is in the last part of the night. If you can be amongst those who remember Allah at that hour, do so*" [At-Tirmidhi, An-Nasaa'ee, and al-Haakim, authentic by Al - Albaani].

Ya Rabb!

I have come to You dripped in humility, sincerity, and vulnerability seeking to be close to You.

It's that time of the night. It's quiet.

Filled with tranquility. And the Presence of my Merciful Rabb

And I want to meet Him.

Shattered, broken, scarred, and in awe of His presence.

I want to tell it all to Him.

Just my Lord and I

It's a journey to Him
So I'll have to prepare for it.
I'll keep my duty to Him
I'll observe my *fard* at the appointed time and keep my
intentions in check
I'll ask Him to help me be consistent with these
appointments.
I yearn to be close to my Merciful Rabb
Never out of His protection
Always in contact.

PART THREE

Dear Soul, Remember Your Lord

21

Why Is This Happening to Me?
by Umm Zakiyyah

وَلَنَبْلُوَنَّكُم بِشَىْءٍ مِّنَ ٱلْخَوْفِ وَٱلْجُوعِ وَنَقْصٍ مِّنَ ٱلْأَمْوَلِ وَٱلْأَنفُسِ وَٱلثَّمَرَٰتِ وَبَشِّرِ ٱلصَّٰبِرِينَ ۝

"And We will surely test you with something of fear and hunger and a loss of wealth and lives and fruits, but give good tidings to the Saabiroon (the people of sabr, who patiently persevere)."
—Al-Baqarah, 2:155

Because *this earth is not your home.*
That's why this is happening to you.
You are not being punished.
You are being chosen.
So don't lower your head in shame.
Except in sujood to your Merciful Creator, Who saw so much beauty and strength in your imperfect heart that He chose you to carry this blessed burden for the purification of your soul.
And He removed from you the burden of people's approval so that you would seek approval only from Him.
So keep going, dear gentle soul.
And ignore the chatter and whispers of those who can only understand your path through their own unhealed wounds, unmet needs, and unhealthy worldly attachments.

Their words might be hurting your heart, but they're lightening your load—as each utterance earns you good deeds and removes some of your sins.

So be patient, dear gentle soul.

Until Jannah.

You're one breath closer already.

And do not grieve too deeply the loss of what was never yours, and do not be too distressed over those who can see only the dirt on your path. Yet your aching feet are walking upon the beautiful path that your Merciful Rabb has paved for you as your customized road toward Him. He already promised you that Jannah will be surrounded by hardships. This is yours.

So do not despair, dear soul. There is more than light at the end of this tunnel.

Yes, there might be more struggle and more pain along this path. But, bi'idhnillaah, there will also be more joy and pleasure, too.

But even still, stay focused, and don't get distracted.

This world was never meant to be your final home.

22

Run to Your Merciful Rabb
by Hajara Salihu

"So, flee to Allah. Indeed, I am to you from Him a clear warner."
—Adh-Dhaariyaat, 51:52

Dear beautiful soul,
Remember this: You are not going to earn Jannah by waking up to it. You are going to strive for it. In your words, deeds, and actions with sincerity seeking the face of your Merciful Rabb.

Remember this: Allah asks nothing from you except that you worship Him without associating partner with Him. Dear Soul, you are the ever needing. Even in your frailty, go to your Lord. Worship Him alone.

How Merciful is your Lord that He'll give you when you seek? He'll forgive you when you sin and repent. He'll reward your good intentions in manifolds and ask that you only worship Him.

SubhanAllah!

Remember this, your Lord doesn't ask for perfection. Perfection belongs to Him alone.

Dear Beautiful Soul, run. Run to your Merciful Rabb with sincerity in your heart.

23

Nothing Is Worthy of Worship But Him
by Layla Graham

ذَلِكُمُ ٱللَّهُ رَبُّكُمْ لَا إِلَهَ إِلَّا هُوَ خَالِقُ كُلِّ شَيْءٍ فَٱعْبُدُوهُ وَهُوَ عَلَى كُلِّ شَيْءٍ وَكِيلٌ ۞

"Such is Allah, your Lord! Laa ilaaha illa Huwa (none has the right to be worshipped but He), the Creator of all things. So worship Him (Alone), and He is the Wakil (Trustee, Disposer of affairs, Guardian, etc.) over all things."
—Al-An'aam, 6:102

Dear beautiful soul,
Remember when you thought you were dying and the only thing you could think to say is *Laa ilaaha illah Allah?* How it comforted you knowing there is no one in existence in the vast arena of creation that knows what you've endured more than God? When you remember that Allah, the only One you worshiped all these years, was hearing you remember Him in such a desperate time? That there is such a beautiful simplicity to faith? Such lovely ease to Tawheed?

There is no one worthy of worship but Allah.

The One. True. God.

24

Remembrance of Allah Through the Recitation of a Beloved Treasure
by Safiyyah Shakir

هُوَ ٱللَّهُ ٱلَّذِى لَآ إِلَٰهَ إِلَّا هُوَ عَٰلِمُ ٱلْغَيْبِ وَٱلشَّهَٰدَةِ هُوَ ٱلرَّحْمَٰنُ ٱلرَّحِيمُ ﴿٢٢﴾ هُوَ ٱللَّهُ ٱلَّذِى لَآ إِلَٰهَ إِلَّا هُوَ ٱلْمَلِكُ ٱلْقُدُّوسُ ٱلسَّلَٰمُ ٱلْمُؤْمِنُ ٱلْمُهَيْمِنُ ٱلْعَزِيزُ ٱلْجَبَّارُ ٱلْمُتَكَبِّرُ سُبْحَٰنَ ٱللَّهِ عَمَّا يُشْرِكُونَ ﴿٢٣﴾ هُوَ ٱللَّهُ ٱلْخَٰلِقُ ٱلْبَارِئُ ٱلْمُصَوِّرُ لَهُ ٱلْأَسْمَآءُ ٱلْحُسْنَىٰ يُسَبِّحُ لَهُ مَا فِى ٱلسَّمَٰوَٰتِ وَٱلْأَرْضِ وَهُوَ ٱلْعَزِيزُ ٱلْحَكِيمُ ﴿٢٤﴾

"He is Allah—there is none worthy of worship except Him: Knower of the seen and unseen. He is the Most Compassionate, Most Merciful. He is Allah—there is no god except Him: the King, the Most Holy, the All-Perfect, the Source of Serenity, the Watcher [of all], the Almighty, the Supreme in Might, the Majestic. Glorified is Allah far above what they associate with Him [in worship]! He is Allah: the Creator, the Inventor, the Shaper. He [alone] has the Most Beautiful Names. Whatever is in the heavens and the earth [constantly] glorifies Him. And He is the Almighty, All-Wise."
—*Al-Hashr, 59:22-24*

How great is the Majesty of Allah?
How great is the Majesty of Allah?
How great is the majesty of Allah?
Glory be to He who sent these words down as a reminder
to His servants of His ownership over all creation. Glory
be to He who granted us the light of Al-Islam.
Glory be to He the treasurer of all treasures. Glory be to
Allah for the gift of memory.
These verses are a treasure to me for only one reason. They
are the only verses I can remember hearing a beloved one
recite before they passed some time ago.
I have various memories of my grandmother. I remember
her smile, her laugh, her tears. I remember the way rooms
would light up when she entered. I remember the
sleepovers my siblings and I had at her place. I remember
the gifts she'd give. Like the gold ring with red ruby that I
treasured from her until I lost it in the toilet. I remember
the day my dad rushed out of the apartment after receiving
a call that she was going to the hospital after throwing up
blood.
I remember being told that she had lung cancer and the
ignorance I had of just how little time we had left with her.
I remember the announcement of her being in remission
and that feeling that we were in the clear; that she wasn't
going anywhere for a long time yet. I remember cursing
that science paper that I chose to write on the various kinds
of cancers out there.
I remember the feeling of dread in my gut as I wrote about
the very small chances of a person surviving brain cancer.
Then came the call that she'd been hospitalized. And again
the call that the cancer was spreading. And again, the call to
make Dua. And again the call that she was blessed to have
her husband around her while he heard her say "La Ilaha
Ilal law." Over and over until her soul left her body.

I remember the way my mother tried to turn away from me and quickly close the bedroom door as she received numerous calls. I remember how my world came crashing down around me, crying at the entrance of the bathroom that stood right across from my mother's room. At the time, she had not yet passed. Yet my soul felt her leaving and something told me it was only a matter of time.

The next morning was New Year's Day of 2011. She passed on the night of December 31st, 2010. My mother came into the room, while my father stood at the entrance. My sister and I were already crying as we knew what they came to say. My father had to turn away. The reality that his mother was no longer with us and just how sad his children, her grandchildren, were at her passing was a lot to bear.

I remember all of this vividly. She was an intricate part of our family. A glue that kept us together. She was the only Muslim grandmother we had. A blessing from Allah though I didn't realize it at the time. To this day, no other grandparent (by blood) has become Muslim. So, I treasure these memories of her. One of those treasures are the last three verses of Surah Hashr that she recited. I do not remember the date except that it was during her time of remission. I remember she was excited to recite them as she led us in one of the evening prayers we recited aloud. I remember her voice as she stuttered on the verses she'd just learned from her teacher. Her voice cracked as tears fell from her eyes.

"He is God There is no God worthy of worship except Him. Knower of the seen and unseen. He is the most compassionate Most Merciful. He is God there is no god except him the king, the most holy, the all-perfect, the source of serenity, the water of all, the majestic Glorified is God far above what they associate with him. He is God the

Creator, the inventor, the shaper he alone has the most beautiful names. Whatever is in the heavens and the earth glorifies him. And he is the almighty all wise."
How wonderful is the mercy of Allah?
How wonderful is the mercy of Allah?
How wonderful is the mercy of Allah?
I think of this when I hear someone recite these verses. Not for the meaning, but for the fact that the only memory I have of my grandmother reciting the Quran, are verses that speak of the majesty of our lord.
This a memory I cherish because, in his mercy, he used her to leave me with a strong memory of her worshipping him. I remember her getting choked up when reciting these verses. There were several times that she'd cried during prayer. But here, she cried because of the beauty in how Allah described himself to his servants. Here she cried because she believed wholeheartedly with every fiber of her being in her creator. Here she cried because he'd brought her from a life that displeased him and gave her the greatest second chance at life there is. He is the most merciful. His mercy allowed her to become a Muslim and help her son and daughter (in-law) in raising Muslim grandchildren.
I miss her a lot. I miss hearing her laugh. The laugh that my father has. I miss seeing her smile. The smile my father now wears. I miss hearing her voice. The voice my father speaks with though deeper – more masculine. I miss the kindness in her eyes. The same love and kindness my father has. My father is my Memukka's child through and through; wise, kind, loving, and generous. Always minding their own business and trying to be understanding of the changing times.
Sometimes I wonder, what her reaction would be like, to this very rapidly changing world. The conversations we would have had, had Allah chosen for her the path of life.

Yet she lived fifty-odd years of life. Full of ups and downs. And He chose for her later years of life to be that of His beloved slave and servant. For that, I can only thank Him.
Ya Allah, the love that my grandmother had for you; I pray that you bless me with the same.
Ya Allah the absolute faith that my grandmother had in you; I pray that you bless me with the same.
Ya Allah, Lord of the seen and unseen, King of kings, the most majestic, most merciful, most generous, and most kind. Protect my grandmother from the punishment of the grave, expand her place in the grave, and allow for this dua to be a sadaqah Jariyah for her from anyone who reads this and sincerely prays for her.

25

Trust Allah and Let Go
by Rasheedah Adisa

وَلَا تَسْتَوِى ٱلْحَسَنَةُ وَلَا ٱلسَّيِّئَةُ ٱدْفَعْ بِٱلَّتِى هِىَ أَحْسَنُ فَإِذَا ٱلَّذِى بَيْنَكَ وَبَيْنَهُ عَدَاوَةٌ كَأَنَّهُ وَلِىٌّ حَمِيمٌ ﴿٣٤﴾

*"And not equal are the good deed and the bad. Repel [evil] by that
[deed] which is better, and thereupon the one whom between you and
him is enmity [will become] as though he was a devoted friend."*
—*Fussilat, 41:34*

وَٱلَّذِينَ ءَامَنُوا۟ وَعَمِلُوا۟ ٱلصَّٰلِحَٰتِ سَنُدْخِلُهُمْ جَنَّٰتٍ تَجْرِى مِن تَحْتِهَا ٱلْأَنْهَٰرُ خَٰلِدِينَ فِيهَآ أَبَدًا وَعْدَ ٱللَّهِ حَقًّا وَمَنْ أَصْدَقُ مِنَ ٱللَّهِ قِيلًا ﴿١٢٢﴾

*"And those who believe and do good, We will soon admit them into
Gardens under which rivers flow, to stay there forever and ever.
Allah's promise is [always] true. And whose word is more truthful
than Allah's?"*
—*An-Nisaa, 4:122*

My friend said - trust Allah and let go.
The words stung with such renewed force.
I struggled so hard to understand its real
meaning.
And more importantly how it applied to me.

"But But But Allah said to strive", I protest,
But the hadith said to "seek what benefits me, to put my
trust in Allah, and to not give up",
But, 'Ya Rabb, my intentions are true'.
I really do not understand.
*"Is there such a thing as giving up something seemingly good for the
sake of Allah??"*, I wrote in my journal.

Truthfully, there are times I still wonder about that
question
Not finding a suitable answer to soothe my heart fully
Then one day, I speak with my dad
And I express my confusion
I tell him I do not understand how being intercepted from
good can be any good.
My dad sighed and said:
"Well, sometimes you have got to choose between a greater
good and the one in front of you".
Sometimes you have to choose between speaking 'good'
and maintaining peace and flexing your correctness or
authority on a matter.
Sometimes you have to choose between silent yet active
persistence over loud criticism and claiming rights.
Sometimes you have to defer to Allah because you fear a
greater sin.
It does not mean you are wrong (if in that situation you
really intend good or are being hurt).
Plus, the reward for your intentions will be recorded.
But you've got to learn to let go and let Allah.
He will come through in a way that befits Him!

I pause finally understanding what it means
I remember the story of the treaty of Hudaybiyah.

This story gave me so much clarity and helped me through some of my trials,
The one where Prophet Mohammed (SAW) saw a dream about going for Umrah,
And acted on it like he was supposed to.
Only to meet interference by the opposition,
And despite his genuinely aggravated companions wanting otherwise
Despite their feeling so insulted by the opposition's demands, genuinely so too
He chose to sign the treaty of Hudaybiyah.
And they had to turn back from experiencing Umrah that year.

They did experience Umrah and Hajj eventually,
Just not that year
And they experienced it with a grander victory
But do not forget they did the work - both times
They took action - both times.
Because you really do not always know if/when the time is exactly right.
Sometimes deferring to the greater good may be what is best for the situation.
Trusting Allah and leaving the matter in His care because you know His time is better.
His ways are better.
And no good you intend or do will go to waste.

So dear heart,
Hand it over.
He will sort it out.
It will eventually make sense.

P.S. This is not a one-answer-fits-all topic and may differ across circumstances.
So, if you ever find yourself in a situation where you have to resort to more direct means.
If you wonder if that is what is best for that situation.
Seek the help and guidance of Allah.
And do what you need to.
Rest assured that your Lord is just and loves truth and justice.
He will never be on the side of injustice or oppression.
He knows and sees all you do.

26

Shattered, Tattered, Battered, and Bruised
by Safiyyah Shakir

۞ أَلَمْ يَأْنِ لِلَّذِينَ ءَامَنُوٓا۟ أَن تَخْشَعَ قُلُوبُهُمْ لِذِكْرِ ٱللَّهِ وَمَا نَزَلَ مِنَ ٱلْحَقِّ وَلَا يَكُونُوا۟ كَٱلَّذِينَ أُوتُوا۟ ٱلْكِتَٰبَ مِن قَبْلُ فَطَالَ عَلَيْهِمُ ٱلْأَمَدُ فَقَسَتْ قُلُوبُهُمْ وَكَثِيرٌ مِّنْهُمْ فَٰسِقُونَ ﴿١٦﴾

ٱعْلَمُوٓا۟ أَنَّ ٱللَّهَ يُحْىِ ٱلْأَرْضَ بَعْدَ مَوْتِهَا قَدْ بَيَّنَّا لَكُمُ ٱلْءَايَٰتِ لَعَلَّكُمْ تَعْقِلُونَ ﴿١٧﴾

"Has the time not yet come for believers' hearts to be humbled at the remembrance of Allah and what has been revealed of the truth, and not be like those given the Scripture before—[those] who were spoiled for so long that their hearts became hardened. And many of them are [still] rebellious. Know that Allah revives the earth after its death.[1] We have certainly made the signs clear for you so perhaps you will understand."
—*Al-Hadeed, 57:16-17*

The following entry I'd written a couple of days before my birthday. It felt incomplete because I couldn't think of any Quranic verses that were an answer to what I had written. Then in our Taddabur Class on October 9th, Ustadha Umm Zakiyyah mentioned Aya 16 and 17 of Surah Hadid. I searched for the meaning of these beautiful and had to send up a prayer of thanks to Allah. How beautiful are the words of His Holy Book?

For several years, I've felt as though my heart is black; hardened to the love of the beautiful deen of Islam. My parents followed the prophetic Sunnah of teaching their children to pray at 7 years of age. My struggles with deen started then. From the age of 7 until the age of 26, I have struggled with feeling any kind of love for the religion of Islam. So much so that it has affected how I view myself when I am alone and when I am around others.

There are times when I feel like a true Muslim. But those times are far and few in between. Most times I feel like a two-faced liar, putting on a show for others. Because I wear the Hijab and Niqab I have to act the part of being a Muslim in public. Yet in private I want to scream and shout at the top of my lungs that I cannot feel a single ounce of anything in my heart and I am afraid. I am afraid for my soul when it's time comes to travel through the Barzakh. I am afraid for my soul when the time comes for me to answer the questions of the Grave. I am afraid for my soul when is stand before Allah on the Day of Judgement.

Over the last two months, I have found myself reflecting on the last 26 years of my life. It has gotten to the point that most nights sleep evades me because of these thoughts. I know that Allah wants me to realize something. I feel it in my soul, yet I cannot see what it is. Mainly my reflections fall on where I am now and where I would like to be in life.
I think about my journey with my Hifz; how I have started and stopped so many times. I could be a Hafitha now had I not stopped completely back in 2016. Yet Allah had other plans for me then.

I think about how I could be graduating with my bachelor's this year (2022) had I not stopped going to school full-time.

I think about how In Sha Allah, I will be 26 in a few days (September 8th). How I had so many plans for where I wanted to be by now; and yet I am nowhere near where I want to be. To be honest, where I am now in life would have completely blindsided my younger self.

The younger me never would have imagined the older me running away from my soul.

The younger me never would have imagined suffering from a deep depression for most of my teens and twenties.

The younger me never would have imagined the painful struggle to overcome depression (mostly).

The younger me never would have imagined having to face a soul so tattered, shattered, and broken that trying to pick up the pieces and put them back together feels like putting together a jigsaw puzzle.

The younger me never imagined going through the painful and quiet struggle of trying to hold on to that little white dot of faith in an ocean of blackness.

The me I am today now realizes that those tests were the start of a long and arduous fight to get back to him. Some days go by with ease. Most go by with every ounce of my being screaming at me to fight harder: try harder.

Yet here I am still at the doorstep of the path I know to follow. A hesitant foot rising slower than a sloth's movement, to take the first step along that path. Mouth visibly sewn shut so the tongue cannot move in remembrance of its creator. Muffled voices wanting to scream out words the soul desperately wants the heart to believe.

Laa illaaha illa Allah!
Laa illaaha illa Allah!
Laa illaaha illa Allah!

If only the dark and black empty space that once housed a beating heart would allow those words to penetrate. There are sweet yet hard lessons to learn from these tests. Now it's time for me to begin in sincere earnest my journey back to him. I am thankful, grateful, and sorrowful.

Thankful for the tests that brought me to where I am now.

Grateful for the lessons learned along the way.

Sorrowful for the fact I'm still nowhere near where I want to be.

I may not be where I want to be, but I am where Allah sees is best for me. I am at the very beginning where every day I have to say *Laa illaaha illa Allah* out loud, whispered, or in my head, just to feel a beat from my heart; and lighten the pain of carrying an organ of my body, the mirror of my soul, that I cannot hear or feel.

لَّآ إِلَـٰهَ إِلَّآ أَنتَ سُبْحَـٰنَكَ إِنِّى كُنتُ مِنَ ٱلظَّـٰلِمِينَ

"There is no god ˹worthy of worship˺ except You. Glory be to You! I have certainly done wrong."
Surah Al-Anbiyaa, Verse 87

PART FOUR
Finding Your Way Back to Allah

27

Be Ready
by Umm Zakiyyah

وَبَشِّرِ ٱلَّذِينَ ءَامَنُواْ وَعَمِلُواْ ٱلصَّٰلِحَٰتِ أَنَّ لَهُمْ جَنَّٰتٍ تَجْرِى مِن تَحْتِهَا ٱلْأَنْهَٰرُ كُلَّمَا رُزِقُواْ مِنْهَا مِن ثَمَرَةٍ رِّزْقًا قَالُواْ هَٰذَا ٱلَّذِى رُزِقْنَا مِن قَبْلُ وَأُتُواْ بِهِۦ مُتَشَٰبِهًا وَلَهُمْ فِيهَآ أَزْوَٰجٌ مُّطَهَّرَةٌ وَهُمْ فِيهَا خَٰلِدُونَ ﴿٢٥﴾

"And give glad tidings to those who believe and do righteous deeds that they will have gardens [in Paradise] beneath which rivers flow. Whenever they are provided with a provision of fruit therefrom, they will say, 'This is what we were provided with before.' And it is given to them in likeness. And they will have therein purified spouses, and they will abide therein eternally."
—*Al-Baqarah*, 2:45

Here's something I learned on my journey of healing: *Growth can feel like a setback when the weight of self-awareness settles on your soul.*

It's like the saying, "It gets worse before it gets better." But here's the truth: It just *feels* worse before it gets better—and it also feels worse *while* it gets better.

Why? Because healing hurts.

This is true when you are healing a physical injury, and it is equally true when you are healing an emotional injury.

Just like healing in physical therapy requires careful attention and painful exercise at the site of injury, so it is with emotional healing. And when that injury is in your heart or soul, the pain is all the more deeply felt.

But so is the relief.

So is the joy.

And so is the beautiful light that will shine from your soul, bi'idhnillaah, at the very place you thought would be your undoing.

This, because you never gave up on your personal growth, even when the work itself felt like a setback.

So smile, my love, and be grateful. You are not moving backwards. Your Merciful Rabb is only pulling you back in preparation to launch you farther than you've ever gone before.

Be ready.

28

For the Beautiful, Imperfectly Perfect Soul
by Safiyyah Shakir

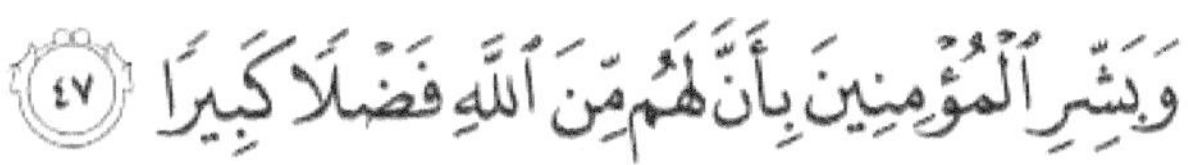

"And give good tidings to the believer that they will have from Allah a great bounty."
—*Al-Ahzaab*, 33:47

Dear Beautiful, Imperfectly Perfect Soul,
I see you. I hear you. I understand. The struggle is real. Holding on to our *emaan* in this day and age is like holding on to hot coal. Everywhere you look *haram* stares you in the face. *Shaytaan* delighting in the struggle of those lost souls. Yet that isn't you. Because you my dear beautiful imperfect soul understand that Allah wants you to struggle to turn back to him. So keep going!
Keep going!
Keep going!
Keep going!
Remember that this life is a test And Allah only gives what He knows we can take on. The goal is us turning to him in aid for when things go bad and to turn to him in gratefulness when things are going ok. Take heed in these words Allah has revealed to you and me and keep going. We are going to fall short some days and on others feel as though we are on top of the world. So, place your forehead

and nose on the ground and allow those tears to flow. Do not be ashamed of crying for tears are a mercy from Allah! Call out to your lord for His help, His mercy, and His forgiveness. Do not lose hope for we are all in this together!

May Allah grant all your prayers for forgiveness, grant you his mercy, ease your hardships, and increase your *emaan* to bounds that you yourself could not fathom. May Allah protect you from all that is evil in this world, the hardships of the grave, and grant you shade on the Day of Judgement. May you be of those who are given glad tidings on that Day of the great bounty from your Lord and Creator.

29

Navigating Your Way Home
by Shazia Abdullah Ahmed

On Sunday, August 8th, 2021, Our Beautiful Qur'an Journey hosted a live Tadabbur event with special guest, Dr. Shaakira, who shared her journey of losing her way and finding her way back to Allah after a life of sin. This Qur'anic reflection is inspired by that session.

إِلَّا مَن تَابَ وَءَامَنَ وَعَمِلَ عَمَلًا صَلِحًا فَأُوْلَـٰٓئِكَ يُبَدِّلُ ٱللَّهُ سَيِّـَٔاتِهِمْ حَسَنَـٰتٍ وَكَانَ ٱللَّهُ غَفُورًا رَّحِيمًا ﴿٧٠﴾

"As for those who repent, believe, and do good deeds, they are the ones whose evil deeds Allah will change into good deeds. For Allah is All-Forgiving, Most Merciful."
—Al-Furqaan, 25:70

The analogy on how we can navigate back to the path of guidance and strive in the way of Allah hit home for me. Dr. Shaakira said that when we're going somewhere, we use GPS to track our route and if by any chance we deviate from the track we go back to the GPS to reach the right destination. Our destination is Jannah and we often lose our way while striving to reach this destination. In times like these, we need to remember that turning to Allah SWT, and keeping with His commandments through Qur'an and Sunnah is our GPS to returning to the path that will lead us to our destination in shaa Allah.

My Dear beautiful soul, I want you to remember this every time you lose your way and struggle, you just need to reroute your destination using the GPS given to us by Allah SWT and you will find your way back to Him in shaa Allah.

إِلَّا مَن تَابَ وَءَامَنَ وَعَمِلَ عَمَلًا صَـٰلِحًا فَأُوْلَـٰٓئِكَ يُبَدِّلُ ٱللَّهُ سَيِّئَاتِهِمْ حَسَنَـٰتٍ ۗ وَكَانَ ٱللَّهُ غَفُورًا رَّحِيمًا

As for those who repent, believe, and do good deeds, they are the ones whose evil deeds Allah will change into good deeds. For Allah is All-Forgiving, Most Merciful. (Surah Furqan, Aayah 70)

Sr Baiyinah (Ustadha Umm Zakiyyah) mentioned in the explanation of the above *Aayah* that the word *"Yubaddil"* means that something is there and that thing itself is changed into something else. Some people sin, and yes Allah SWT forgives them, however, He does something more, He takes the sin that they did and changes the actual sin into good deeds. How is this possible? It's like once a person is sincere in their regret, and they don't just ask for forgiveness but take the lesson from the sin and help others come back to Allah (SWT) that bad deed they experienced is turned into their good deed because now they're helping others to stay away from it. It made me reflect on how Allah (SWT) guided Sr Shaakira to the path of helping others who are going through a similar situation she had been through, how her dedication to helping others with her skills is a sign of acceptance of repentance, and Allah (SWT) changing a bad deed to a good one Subhaan Allah!

My Dear beautiful soul, you have an example in this life story to look into your own actions and think of what mistakes you have made in life and how helping yourself and others overcome it can be a path to true repentance and *Ridaa* of Allah (SWT) in shaa Allah.

One more point of reflection from this session is that *shaytaan* will come in the form of humans, or internal whispers trying to remind us of our sins and how we're not worthy of Allah (SWT's)Love, but we need to remember through this *Aayah* that what *shaytaan* says and whispers inside of us is a lie, because Allah (SWT) Himself has told us through this *Aayah* that He will indeed forgive us if we repent, believe, and do good deeds.

My Dear Beautiful soul, do not fear *Shaytaan's* false whispers if you have wronged yourself by sinning because Allah (SWT) says in the Qur'an:

قُلْ يَـٰعِبَادِىَ ٱلَّذِينَ أَسْرَفُوا۟ عَلَىٰٓ أَنفُسِهِمْ لَا تَقْنَطُوا۟ مِن رَّحْمَةِ ٱللَّهِ ۚ إِنَّ ٱللَّهَ ۞ يَغْفِرُ ٱلذُّنُوبَ جَمِيعًا ۚ إِنَّهُۥ هُوَ ٱلْغَفُورُ ٱلرَّحِيمُ

Say, ˹O Prophet, that Allah says,˺ "O My servants who have exceeded the limits against their souls! Do not lose hope in Allah's mercy, for Allah certainly forgives all sins.1 He is indeed the All-Forgiving, Most Merciful. (Surah Az Zumar,: 53)

30

Read!

by Safiyyah Shakir

بِسْمِ ٱللَّهِ ٱلرَّحْمَٰنِ ٱلرَّحِيمِ

ٱقْرَأْ بِٱسْمِ رَبِّكَ ٱلَّذِى خَلَقَ ﴿١﴾

خَلَقَ ٱلْإِنسَٰنَ مِنْ عَلَقٍ ﴿٢﴾

ٱقْرَأْ وَرَبُّكَ ٱلْأَكْرَمُ ﴿٣﴾

ٱلَّذِى عَلَّمَ بِٱلْقَلَمِ ﴿٤﴾

عَلَّمَ ٱلْإِنسَٰنَ مَا لَمْ يَعْلَمْ ﴿٥﴾

"Read, in the Name of your Lord Who Created humans from a clinging clot. Read! And your Lord is the Most Generous, who taught by the pen humanity what they knew not."
—*Al-'Alaq, 96:1-5*

These are the first words of the Quran revealed to Prophet Muhammad (Peace and Blessings be Upon Him). A story that is taught in Islamic schools everywhere. I remember hearing it from my mother when I was a child. The story of how Prophet Muhammad (Peace and Blessings be Upon Him) came to know of his being chosen to be the last Prophet of Allah. How Angel Jibril came to the Prophet (Peace and Blessings be Upon him) in the Cave of Hira. Revealing to him that Allah had chosen him to be a Prophet. For a long time, to me, these verses were important only because they were the first to be revealed in the Quran. This past summer, I was shown another reason on why these verses are so important.

I made my intentions during Ramadan, that I would read the Quran in its entirety in English. That plan never came to fruition. Looking back, I realize why. I made all the excuses to not pick my English translation. Finally, I had to admit to myself the biggest truth I did not want to face. I am afraid of knowing what my Lord has to say to me in this book.

SubhanAllah, I want to be among those who memorized the Quran. I want the blessing of being told on the day of Judgement to "recite and ascend" and yet I cannot even pick up the blessing Allah gave to the Muslims who do not speak or understand Arabic. An English translation that tells the meaning or is as close to the Arabic meaning as possible. I could not pick it up without being afraid of what I would see. How empty is this vessel which Allah has given me? The fight with my soul is such that I was comfortable with only reciting his words in Arabic and not trying to even know what He was saying.

This battle continued until my family traveled to DC in July. I read the entirety of Surah Fatiha and Surah Baqarah from beginning to end in two days. When I returned from vacation, I completed Surah Imran and a portion of Surah Nisaa. Life happened and I would make my intentions to pick up my book again, but I didn't. I did not read anything else until I and another Soul sister started to implement a tradition of reading a portion of Surah Baqarah in Arabic and English every night before we went to sleep. That was the only time I made the effort to read.

Now that we are on a short break, I think about how once the break started, I stopped reading again. I think of how, when I first opened the book and started to read, I felt something ignite in my soul. I felt my heartbeat for the first time in a long time. I heard the word "read" echo in my mind every night and day. It was like I'd awakened this feeling of desperation to grab my English translation and read. I knew I was being told to continue the path I'd started. To be honest, I am afraid to continue. That fear of reading the meaning of Allah's words is still strong within me.

If the greatest man that ever lived could answer the call of God from that one word. If thousands of beautiful souls could answer the call from that one word and learn the meaning behind every letter that Allah revealed to mankind. What excuse do I, a seed in an ocean of beautiful orchids, have in not picking up my book in English and reading His words in a language that I do understand?

"Read!" This word was once a strong echo in my mind. I heard it when I saw my book in my bag. I heard it when I saw it on the table. I heard it when I saw it on my bed. I heard it when I saw it on my bookshelf. Loud and clear, "Open the book that your lord has blessed you with and read!" But I have yet to pick it up again. And now the echo has died away. Thinking on it a part of me fears, "have I been forsaken by my lord?"

No... I just need to finally listen; to open my book and read again. I hear You, Ya Allah. I make my intention to start again and read.

31

I Am Still Here
by Aminah H.

رَبَّنَا لَا تُزِغْ قُلُوبَنَا بَعْدَ إِذْ هَدَيْتَنَا وَهَبْ لَنَا مِن لَّدُنكَ رَحْمَةً إِنَّكَ أَنتَ ٱلْوَهَّابُ ﴿٨﴾

"[They say] 'Our Lord! Do not let our hearts deviate after you have guided us. Grant us Your mercy. You are indeed the Giver [of all bounties].'"
—*Ali 'Imraan, 3:8*

A voice says, 'I am still here. Still here waiting for you. Is that my voice I hear? Or is that the voice of Allah speaking to me? Sometimes it is hard to tell. Are you waiting, O Allah, for me to put my worlds together and marry as one? It seems like, for so many years, I have been trying to put my worlds together. Time seems to be moving faster than ever! I can feel it moving, spinning sometimes out of control. Sometimes I have been so close to pulling it together; in a way where I think I will have your favor. But it does not seem like I can get it right. I keep moving in the same spot…. but I keep moving.

I am grateful beyond words. Happiness comes and goes. I have everything I need, but I still feel empty inside; still feel caught in a cage. Sometimes, I don't feel whole but God, I want to be! Another possession will not do. Sometimes I feel bound by two worlds. One world feels like the world of nothingness and the other is full of somethingness. My spaces are full, but I feel empty. But still, I am still here. I will be still waiting for You knowing that You are already here.

O Allah, please let my heart not deviate after you have guided me. Please grant me mercy from your own presence for you are the grantor of bounties without measure.

32

Don't Underestimate Your Blessings
by Halima Alisa Diallo

وَإِن تَعُدُّواْ نِعْمَةَ ٱللَّهِ لَا تُحْصُوهَآ إِنَّ ٱللَّهَ لَغَفُورٌ رَّحِيمٌ ١٨

"And if you would count the graces [or favors] of Allah, never would you be able to count them. Truly! Allah is Oft-Forgiving, Most Merciful."
—*An-Nahl*, 16:18

God will use you in unexpected ways! Don't underestimate your blessings!

This is all I can think of when I had to use my discretion to help save someone from being harmed or even worse.

I was thinking about what I should write for my Passion Project journal entry.

I think this will hit home for so many…

I did not know Ms. Doris was confused and lost at first, but after listening to her for five minutes I knew I had to help this lady that could have been my own mother or grandmother to be reunited with her family safe and unharmed.

Ms. Doris had the sweetest face and was a little petite lady in her eighties to nineties I would say. She asked me as I boarded the C train to head home.

She asked me if I knew of a town in Barbados where she was originally from. I told her I did not, but I knew I had to help Ms. Doris.

I took her to the agent to get assistance. The police were called after the location was not coming up on the computer.

I asked Ms. Doris if she has the phone or number of someone she knew. She said no but by the grace and mercy of Allah the police found a number of a family member on a card in her pocketbook.

Alhamdulillah, the family member was contacted and informed of where Ms. Doris was currently and where she can be picked up at.

I accompanied Ms. Doris to the precinct to wait for her relative to arrive.

We had a good conversation while waiting.

I am happy and blessed that I was able to help Ms. Doris to be reunited with her family member.

The family member was very grateful that Ms. Doris was safe and was not harmed.

God used me in a way that was unexpected.

But to me, it was a blessing that was not to be underestimated.

33

Put Your Trust in Allah and Don't Give Up

by Rasheedah Adisa

أُوْلَٰٓئِكَ يُسَٰرِعُونَ فِى ٱلْخَيْرَٰتِ وَهُمْ لَهَا سَٰبِقُونَ ٦١

"It is those who hasten to good deeds, and they are foremost in them."
—*Al-Mu'minoon*, 23:61

Abu Huraira reported: The Messenger of Allah (peace and blessings be upon him) said, "The strong believer is more beloved to Allah than the weak believer, but there is goodness in both of them. Be eager for what benefits you, seek help from Allah, and do not be frustrated. If something befalls you, then do not say: If only I had done something else. Rather say: Allah has decreed what he wills. Verily, the phrase 'if only' opens the way for the work of Satan" (Sahih Muslim 2664).

Once during a conversation with a good senior friend of mine, I asked the following -

"How does one know when to give up on a particular situation? At what point does one stop trying towards a task?"

He gave me a beautiful and comprehensive answer and I would like to share a part of it. He said:

"When do you stop trying? There is no one answer, but it is apt to keep trying until God gives you something else to try or until you get the results you desire. If your strength fails you, check up with GOD on what to push and/or how to push better before you try again. Finally, even if you are sure you are at what you should be pushing, "Watch and Pray" - keep your eyes on your goal while you set your heart on God to draw on His strength and wisdom. Your location/goal could be right, but your method/attitude could be wrong."

To be honest, at this point, I really was not sure what answer I was expecting. People and circumstances around me were convincing me to give up on something I considered valuable. And I simply had no strength left. But when I got that response, I could not help but be thankful that at least someone else understood my thoughts. And when I eventually stumbled upon the hadith above, I finally understood why.

Sometimes, I find that I laugh at myself - When a past conviction suddenly re-awakens, and I put in one more effort. It is funny because most times my dominating thought is - are you not tired of trying? Yes, dear heart, are you not tired of trying? But my brain usually counters - perhaps this time will yield!

And the truth is for the most part Allah causes it to yield.

A redirection,

Some more clarity.

A different approach.

One more opportunity to reassess and renew my intention.

A firmer resolve that it is or is not good for me.

One more lesson on what to do differently.

A bit more understanding of how the process works.

One more strategy on how best to go about it.

But I get one more way out.

Or perhaps, a completely different way that I had never stumbled upon before.

So will I ever try again?

Will I continue to work on forming good habits no matter how many times I have failed?

Will I try staying awake after Fajr today after snoozing off yesterday?

Will I try learning Arabic after my failed attempt the other time?

Will I continue to try on the things that matter?

The short answer?

Yes!

If it is inherently good and pleasing to Allah,

If my soul considers it good and nourishing,

If my intentions are true and sincere,

And if Allah guides my heart back to it.

Then I would.

But this time, it would be with the knowledge of all the lessons that I have learned.

And like always, while trusting Him to be my guide and grant me the best outcome.

34

The Value of Time
by Kathryn Khadijah Holmes-Adamu

"Indeed, it is We who sent down the Qur'an and indeed, We will be its guardian."
—*Al-Hijr*, 15:9

Hifdh of the Qur'an has been one of my top goals for decades. Alhamdullilah, it is one goal that I began to take a little more seriously at the beginning of 2022. My usual methodology involved doing revision sessions when the mood struck me.

This changed recently when at the time of Asr prayer, I experienced chest pain that was so strong and heavy that I had to seize all activity and just rest. I told myself, "Maybe it's just a mild discomfort and it'll go away within a short time." However, by Isha prayer time, I had my son drive me to the hospital for evaluation just to make sure there wasn't something serious going on.

After describing my symptoms to the physician, he explained that I was being worked up for Angina and/or Myocardial infarction. As a nurse, translating the meanings of these words is easy. As I translated the words to chest pain and heart attack, the foremost thought in my mind was - I need more time! I need more time for my hifdh of the Qur'an, more time with my family, and time to accomplish other goals. The Hadith of the Prophet Mohammad (pbuh) became personal in my life and carried so much weight when he said the following:

"Take advantage of five before five: your youth before your old age, your health before sickness, your wealth before poverty, your free time before your busyness, and your life before your death" (Shu'ab al-Imān 9767, saheeh by Al-Albaani).

Alhamdullilah, most of the tests are negative. And although the chest pain persists intermittently, it's so much better than it was. I look at time now with a new lens. Every day that I wake up in the morning brings joy to my heart. Walking in my garden and hearing the birds chirp or looking at the sun rise or set, involves a sweetness that almost brings tears to the eyes. And of course, time with family has become too precious to spend on bickering over matters that will lead to a stressful mindset and more negative physical repercussions. The wake-up call has also extended to my diet and abstaining from those food items that were too hard to resist before! The unhealthy items have certainly lost their attraction as consideration of the physical effects of ingesting them, erases their appeal.

But more importantly, my hifdh journey has taken on a new and precious urgency as I finally realize that I DO have an expiration date; a thought that was long forgotten while focusing on the trials and tribulations of this dunia. My memorization sessions have now become my one-on-one sessions with Allah. In addition to memorizing the Qur'an, I also use this time for reflecting and understanding - on a deeper level - the incredible meaning of His message. One new valuable nugget of information that I learned from a classmate in a recent Taddabur course with Umm Zakiyyah, is that in doing hifdh," revision has to be done whether I feel like it or not." Thus, without daily discipline, permanent memorization won't be achieved.

At the age of 65, I sincerely wish that I had done so many things differently in my life. However, I'm learning that everything has a season. Although this trial is painful and scary, I am also grateful for it because, in addition to hopefully having sins removed from my scales, I sincerely believe that Allah is giving me a chance to reset and implement my intention for hifdh that will hopefully make it even better than it was before, InshaAllah!

35

Do Good Deeds
by Hajara Salihu

يُؤْمِنُونَ بِٱللَّهِ وَٱلْيَوْمِ ٱلْأَخِرِ وَيَأْمُرُونَ بِٱلْمَعْرُوفِ وَيَنْهَوْنَ عَنِ ٱلْمُنكَرِ وَيُسَرِعُونَ فِى ٱلْخَيْرَتِ وَأُوْلَٰٓئِكَ مِنَ ٱلصَّٰلِحِينَ ﴿١١٤﴾

"They believe in Allah and the Last Day, and they enjoin what is right and forbid what is wrong and hasten to good deeds. And those are among the righteous."
—Ali 'Imraan, 3:114

Bismillah.
"Do good deeds properly, sincerely, and moderately; and know that your deeds will not make you enter paradise, and that the most beloved deed to Allah is the most regular and constant even if it were little" *(Bukhari).*

Lately, I've been feeling exhausted. This exhaustion has affected every part of my being. It's affected my spirituality too. I find myself rushing through my acts of worship. I make *wudhoo* in a haste. And I'm eager to say the *taslim* just so I can get back to rest because I feel exhausted. On days that I fast, I rarely make *adhkaar* or remember to make dua at the time I break my fast.

As I read this hadith and reflect deeply on it, I realize it is not rest I need (well, maybe a little) what I do need is to practice PAUSE.

Slow it all down.

Pause while making *wudhoo*
Pause after reciting every ayah while making *salaah*
Pause between sujood
Pause before going back to rest after *taslim*
Pause while doing chores
Pause while at work
In the moment of that Pause, I'll find time to make adhkaar
In the moment of that Pause, I'll release the exhaustion.
In the moment of that Pause, I'll renew my intentions
In the Practice of this Pause, I'll begin to do good deeds
properly, with renewed intention and as moderately as I am
able to.
This is self-awareness dear soul.
Now that I know, I'll do better.
 Bi'idhinillah

CLOSING NOTES
Feeling Grateful for Our Beautiful Soul Tribe

"Whoever is not grateful for small things will not be grateful for large things. Whoever is not thankful to people is not thankful to Allah. Mentioning the blessings of Allah is gratitude and ignoring them is ingratitude. Unity is a mercy and division is a punishment."
—Prophet Muhammad, peace and blessings be upon him
(Musnad Aḥmad 17982, saheeh by Al-Albaani)

36

Dear Beautiful Souls
by Umm Zakiyyah

وَمِنْ ءَايَتِهِۦ خَلْقُ ٱلسَّمَوَتِ وَٱلْأَرْضِ وَٱخْتِلَفُ أَلْسِنَتِكُمْ وَأَلْوَنِكُمْ إِنَّ فِى ذَٰلِكَ لَأَيَتٍ لِلْعَلِمِينَ ﴿٢٢﴾

"And of His signs is the creation of the heavens and the earth and the diversity of your languages and your colors. Indeed, in that are signs for those of knowledge."
—*Ar-Room, 30:22*

Today, I'm feeling grateful for the soul tribe of companions in faith that Allah has blessed me with in Our Beautiful Qur'an Journey (Tadabbur). As I get to know each of you beautiful souls, dear sisters, I am reminded of the ayah from Al-Kahf where Allah says:

وَٱصْبِرْ نَفْسَكَ مَعَ ٱلَّذِينَ يَدْعُونَ رَبَّهُم بِٱلْغَدَوٰةِ وَٱلْعَشِىِّ يُرِيدُونَ وَجْهَهُۥ وَلَا تَعْدُ عَيْنَاكَ عَنْهُمْ تُرِيدُ زِينَةَ ٱلْحَيَوٰةِ ٱلدُّنْيَا وَلَا تُطِعْ مَنْ أَغْفَلْنَا قَلْبَهُۥ عَن ذِكْرِنَا وَٱتَّبَعَ هَوَىٰهُ وَكَانَ أَمْرُهُۥ فُرُطًا ﴿٢٨﴾

"And keep yourself patient [by being] with those who call upon their Lord in the morning and the evening, seeking His countenance. And let not your eyes pass beyond them, desiring adornments of the worldly

So, I am not allowing my eyes to overlook you, dear beautiful souls. I am thanking Allah that I met you and that He chose you to be amongst my soul companions in this world.

So, dear beautiful souls, in showing my gratitude for my Merciful Rabb you into my life, here is my prayer for you:

May every trial you face in this confusing world be a means for you to draw closer to your Merciful Creator in this world and in the Hereafter. If your heart is hurting or breaking, may He heal it and grant you tranquility and peace. If you are battling loneliness and are longing for companionship, may He grant you a soul companion who will be a comfort and a mercy to you in this world and your companion in Paradise. If you have suffered loss and have no idea how you'll go on, may He grant you better than you lost and reunite you with the believers amongst His beloved in this world and in the Hereafter.

If you are battling spiritual confusion, emptiness, or frustration, may He gift you with the light of emaan, may He make the coolness of your eye the Salaah, and may He make the spring of your heart the Qur'an until you meet Him.

And for those heartfelt prayers that you've whispered to Him on the edge of desperation, tears in your eyes, begging of His bounty and mercy, may He grant you what your heart desires—and may He grant you better than the best you could hope for or imagine.

And may your last days be the best of your life, your last deeds your best deeds, and your best day the Day you meet Ar-Rahmaan.

And dear beautiful soul, may the Most Merciful write you down amongst those whom He loves, announcing your name above the heavens and commanding the angels to love you as He loves you, until love of you is placed in the hearts of His believers on earth.

About the Instructor and Founder of
Our Beautiful Qur'an Journey (Tadabbur)

Known for her soul-touching books and spiritual reflections on the Qur'an and emotional healing, Umm Zakiyyah is a world-renowned author, teacher, and soul-care mentor.

Also known by her birth name Ruby Moore and her "Muslim name" Baiyinah Siddeeq, Umm Zakiyyah is the internationally acclaimed, award-winning author of more than thirty books, including novels, short stories, and self-help. Her books are used in high schools and universities in the United States and worldwide, and her work has been translated into multiple languages.

Umm Zakiyyah studied Arabic, Qur'an, Islamic sciences, *'aqeedah*, and *tafseer* in America, Egypt, and Saudi Arabia for more than fifteen years. She currently teaches *tajweed* (rules of reciting Qur'an), *tafseer* (explanation of the meaning of the Qur'an), and *tadabbur* (deep reflections on the Qur'an) via uzhearthub.com.

Umm Zakiyyah has a BA degree in Elementary Education, an MA in English Language Learning, and Cambridge's CELTA (Certificate in English Language Teaching to Adults).

She is a certified Rapid Transformational Therapy ® (RTT) practitioner and hypnotherapist currently based in the United States. She is also a certified member of IACT (International Association of Counselors and Therapists) and an executive member of IICT (International Institute of Complementary Therapists).

For information on UZ courses, including Our Beautiful Qur'an Journey (Tadabbur) go to **uzhearthub.com** and **uzuniversity.com**

Connect with Umm Zakiyyah online:
uzauthor.com and **sqsoul.com**
Instagram: @uzauthor

Special Thanks to Our Publishing Team

Executive Publisher: Umm Zakiyyah
She is an internationally acclaimed author, soul-care mentor, and founder of Our Beautiful Qur'an Journey at uzhearthub.com

Project Coordinator: Hajara Salihu
She is a lawyer based in Nigeria with over 10 years experience and is passionate about self -development and fostering interpersonal skills. She is the President/Co-founder of Al- Musaa'id foundation, a non-profit organization working for the well-being and health of less privileged individuals. She seizes any opportunity she has to grow and better herself on the path of righteousness, fairness and honesty.

Assistant Project Coordinator: Naimah B
Currently a Client Advisor with extensive background in buying.

Editor-in-Chief: Shazia Abdullah Ahmed
Ustaadhah Shazia is a daughter, a student of Tajweed Sciences, Practical Tajweed Coach, BeingMe Youth Mentor, Entrepreneur, an upcoming Author and a lifelong learner.

She holds an ijaazah (official certificate) in Tajweed for Qaida Nuraniah from Al-Furqan Group and is a native of India. She graduated from Umm al Qura University in Makkah, Saudi Arabia with a diploma in Arabic language and Islamic Studies, where she earned the award of "Ideal Student of the Year." She also holds a Diploma in Islamic Psychology from Aspire College, has Certifications in Leadership and Personal Development from IOU, and has participated in the Parents and Teachers Training from ERDC.

She is the head instructor and founder of Tabaarak Academy and has worked as a translator and daiyah for the Ministry of Islamic Affairs in Makkah, Saudi Arabia, where she currently resides.

General Project Assistant: Umm Jameelah
Umm Jameelah, revert to Islaam since 2017. Co-authored "I Didn't Want to Become Muslim, Then Snapchat Happened" with Umm Zakiyyah, aspired NYC Henna Artist.

Assistant Editor: Rasheedah Adisa
Rasheedah is a pharmacist, an aspiring psychologist and a budding writer. She is passionate about writing reflective pieces and sharing

empowering stories to inspire positive change and promote spiritual, mental, and emotional health and well-being of people. She loves laughing and listening to meaningful conversations on life experiences and Islam.

Assistant Editor: Safiyyah Shakir

Safiyyah Shakir is beginners Quran Reading and Memorization teacher for children and adults. She has attained an Ijaza in practical Tajweed through Al-Furqaan Group located in Saudi Arabia. Safiyyah currently runs an online platform for children to learn how to read Quran and memorize their first two juz (29, and 30). She is also working on her own Hifdth and hopes to attain an Ijaza in Hafs an Asim and in Theoretical Tajweed.

Assistant Editor: Rafeen Arif

Rafeen Arif is an educator based in Mumbai, India, and has served as a leader in three schools across multiple cities. Her mission is to build and strengthen the Muslim community through education. She chose to be a teacher because it gives her a sense of purpose. Rafeen is a mother of two and likes languages, travelling, and working with groups of people.

Also By Umm Zakiyyah

If I Should Speak

A Voice

Footsteps

Realities of Submission

Hearts We Lost

The Friendship Promise

Muslim Girl

His Other Wife

UZ Short Story Collection

The Test Paper (a children's book)

Pain. From the Journal of Umm Zakiyyah

Broken yet Faithful. From the Journal of Umm Zakiyyah

Faith. From the Journal of Umm Zakiyyah

Let's Talk About Sex and Muslim Love

Reverencing the Wombs That Broke You: A Daughter of Rape and Abuse Inspires Healing and Healthy Family

Prejudice Bones in My Body: Essays on Muslim Racism, Bigotry and Spiritual Abuse

And Then I Gave Up: Essays About Faith and Spiritual Crisis in Islam

I Almost Left Islam: How I Reclaimed My Faith

The Abuse of Forgiveness: Manipulation and Harm in the Name of Emotional Healing

even if. bits and pieces from the heart of Umm Zakiyyah

No One Taught Me the Human Side of Islam: The Muslim Hippie's Story of Living with Bipolar Disorder

He Asked About Islam

Alone, But In the Company of Your Lord

Come Back To Allah, Dear Soul: Salaah Coursebook

Dear Soul, It's Time: A Journey of Coming Back To Allah

I'm Divorced Now: Heartbreak and Healing

What Did You Expect? Lessons on Spiritual Honesty

Dear Struggling Soul: Affirmations for Spiritual Self-Compassion

Nurturing the Nafs: Emotional Honesty for the Female Soul

Learning Love: Self-Care Journal

Salaah Is a Blessing, Not a Burden

Your Lord Has Not Forgotten You: To the Non-Arab Learning Qur'an

Before You Become His Garment in Marriage: Do's and Don'ts for Muslim Women

Glossary of Common Arabic and Islamic Terms

adab: good manners; showing others humble respect; Islamic etiquette

alhamdulillah: "All praise belongs to Allah (God, the Creator) alone"

Allah: Arabic term for God; the only One who has the right to be worshipped

'aqeedah: foundational beliefs of the Islamic spiritual way of life

ayaat: plural form of *ayah*

ayah: verse from Qur'an or divine sign

'ayn: (literally "eye") used in reference to "the evil eye," which is often rooted in harmful envy or unhealthy admiration of someone devoid of mentioning Allah

bid'ah: sinful innovation in religion

bi'idhnillaah: "with the help of Allah (the Creator)"

da'wah: teaching others about Islam; inviting others to spiritual guidance

deen: spiritual way of life; religion

dhikr: sincere mention or remembrance of Allah (the Creator); message; reminder

dhulm: wrongdoing or oppression (of others or one's own soul)

du'aa: prayerful supplication; informal prayer

dunya: this worldly life as opposed to the Hereafter

'ebaadah: sincere worship, submission, and obedience to Allah alone

emaan: sincere faith; authentic spirituality; belief in Islam; *Tawheed*

faahishah: immorality, usually of a sexual nature

faasiq: evildoer; a person living in open sin or wrongdoing

fatwa: Islamic ruling or opinion given by a scholar

fisq: evil, corruption, or clear sin and wrongdoing

fitnah: (plural: *fitan*) difficult trial

fitrah: inherent inborn nature of every human soul to worship Allah alone and to live a spiritually and morally upright life

ghayb: unseen

gheebah: backbiting; saying anything about a fellow Muslim that if they were to hear it, they would dislike it

ghuroor: spiritual self-deception

halaal: divinely blessed or permissible

haraam: divinely forbidden or sinful

harf: a single Arabic letter (plural: *huroof*)

hasad: envy that is sinful and spiritually destructive

hasan: good; often used in reference to the rating of "good" regarding the strength of authenticity of a prophetic hadith

hijrah: migration from one land to another for the sake of your faith; moving from a place that harms the soul to a place that nourishes the soul

hikmah: literally "wisdom"; often used in reference to the divinely inspired prophetic wisdom

iftaar: the moment of breaking one's fast at sunset

ijmaa': unanimous agreement amongst the earliest Muslims and scholars

istighfaar: uttering supplications seeking Allah's forgiveness

Istikhaarah: prayer and supplication for making a decision about something

istislaam: spiritual surrender

jahiliyyah: pre-Islamic days of spiritual and moral ignorance before the prophetic assignment was given to Prophet Muhammad (peace be upon him); any mindset or life path that mirrors this spiritual and moral ignorance

Jahannam: Hellfire (also called Hell)

Jannah: Paradise (also called Heaven)

kaafir: disbeliever; any person who rejects a foundational part of Islam, who knowingly rejects a well-established principle or teaching of Islam, or who knowingly introduces or accepts any teaching that forbids what Allah allows or permits what Allah has forbidden regarding any matter wherein disagreement is not permitted

khaashi'oon: people who are defined by their *khushoo'*; those who are sincerely and humbly submissive in their worship and obedience to Allah

khula': female-initiation marriage dissolution

khushoo': sincerity and humility of the heart and soul; deep concentration in *Salaah* such that the heart is consistently spiritually nourished by its sincere and humble connection to its Creator in every part of prayer

kibr: sinful pride or pride that is spiritually harmful; looking down on others and rejecting the truth

kitaab: literally "book"; often used in reference to the Qur'an (i.e. the Book of Allah)

kufr: disbelief; spiritual blasphemy; any belief, speech or action that cancels one's *emaan*

Laa ilaaha illaa Allah: statement of *Tawheed* or declaration of faith that means, "Nothing has the right to be worshipped except Allah alone"

madhloom: one who has been wronged, oppressed, or suffered from *dhulm*

mahr: obligatory gift given to woman upon marriage; dowry

masjid: (plural: *masaajid*) the house of worship for the Muslim

nafs: inner-self or desires that are self-serving and spiritually harmful

nameemah: gossip or tale-carrying

naseehah: sincere advice offered to inspire soul-nourishment and life betterment in the one being advised

nikaah: Islamic marriage contract; often written and signed before the man and woman live together

qadar: divine decree; predestination

qalb: heart

qawwaam: the man's divinely assigned role of being the maintainer, provider, and protector of women in the home and society

Qiyaam ul-Layl: the blessed night prayer, prayed in last third of night

Rabb: another name for Allah that refers to His Lordship over creation; Creator, Owner and Manager of all that exists

rahmah: divine mercy

rak'ah: one unit of *Salaah* (formal prayer)

riba: usury

riyaa: insincerity; showing off; seeking the pleasure, admiration, reward, or attention of other than Allah

rizq: provision or wealth

ruqyaa': spiritual healing that includes reciting the Qur'an over someone and/or reciting *dhikr* and prayerful supplications for the purpose of healing illness or removing the effects of *'ayn* or *sihr* on someone

sabr: sincere patience; patiently persevering upon that which benefits one's life and soul, and patiently persevering in abstaining from that which harms one's life and the soul

sadaqah: voluntary, non-obligatory charity

sahih/saheeh: authentic; the highest grade of a hadith's authenticity

sajdah: prostrating the forehead on the floor in submission to Allah

Salaah: the five foundational prayers: *Fajr, Dhuhr, 'Asr, Maghrib,* and *'Ishaa';* second pillar of Islam; formal prayer, whether optional or obligatory

sallallaahu'alayhi wa sallam: (ﷺ) prayers of peace and blessing upon the Prophet

shahaadah: formal declaration of faith that marks one's entry into Islam: "I bear witness that nothing has the right to be worshipped except Allah alone, and I bear witness that Muhammad is His slave and messenger"; sincere testimony of *Tawheed* recited repeatedly throughout a Muslim's life

Shaytaan: the devil; Satan

shirk: assigning divine attributes to creation or creation's attributes to the Creator

shukr: sincere gratefulness, thankfulness or gratitude

sihr: often referred to as "black magic": when someone works with the jinn to harm someone or get a specific outcome in this world

soorah/surah: (plural: *suwar*) divine chapter of the Qur'an

SubhaanAllah: statement of glorification of Allah: "Glory to Allah, and Exalted and High is He above any imperfection"

sujood: another term for *sajdah*: prostrating the forehead on the floor in submission to Allah

Sunnah: prophetic guidance or example; the life and teachings of Prophet Muhammad (peace and blessings be upon him)

Sunni: a description of Muslims who affiliate with understanding and living Islam based on the prophetic Sunnah

tafseer: authentic interpretation and spiritual explanation of the *ayaat* of Qur'an

tajweed: rules of reciting the Qur'an based on one or more of the seven authentic prophetic recitation styles

taqwaa: sincere God-consciousness and daily soul care that protects the heart from corruption and the soul from spiritual harm in the Hereafter

tawakkul: sincere trust in the wisdom and decisions of the Creator

tawbah: sincere repentance; turning one's life around as a form of seeking forgiveness for past sins and wrongdoing

Tawheed: Oneness of Allah; singling out the Creator alone in worship; authentic monotheism; sincere belief in the Oneness of Allah

tazkiyyatun-nafs: purification of the soul; spiritual nourishment that is attained through sincerity while fulfilling the required and optional acts of worship in Islam

'ulamaa: scholars; people of spiritual knowledge (plural of *'aalim*)

ummah: all Muslims from every generation; worldwide faith community

uswah: example or pattern to be followed by others

Witr: highly recommended prayer performed after *Ishaa'* or at the closing of *Qiyaam ul-Layl* and consists of three units of prayer (odd number)

wudhoo': ritual ablution that is done before *Salaah*

zakaah/zakaat: obligatory charity paid from one's wealth and given to the needy

zina: fornication or adultery